STUDENT UNIT GUIDE

AS Economics
UNIT 3

AQA

Module 3: Markets at Work

Ray Powell & Richard Swain

Philip Allan Updates, an imprint of Hodder Education, part of Hachette Livre UK, Market Place, Deddington, Oxfordshire OX15 0SE

Orders
Bookpoint Ltd, 130 Milton Park, Abingdon, Oxfordshire, OX14 4SB
tel: 01235 827720
fax: 01235 400454
e-mail: uk.orders@bookpoint.co.uk
Lines are open 9.00 a.m.–5.00 p.m., Monday to Saturday, with a 24-hour message answering service. You can also order through the Philip Allan Updates website: www.philipallan.co.uk

ISBN 978-0-86003-479-7

Printed by MPG Books, Bodmin

Hachette Livre UK's policy is to use papers that are natural, renewable and recyclable products and made from wood grown in sustainable forests. The logging and manufacturing processes are expected to conform to the environmental regulations of the country of origin.

P00999

proved to be the most popular. The environment option has been the second most popular option. Relatively few schools and colleges have prepared their students for the economics of sport and leisure.

If you have prepared for only one of the three options, then you *must* answer the question set on that option. Don't bother even to look at the other two questions — you will be wasting valuable examination time! If you have prepared for two of the three options, you should read all the data and look carefully at all the parts of both questions, paying special attention to the last part of each question. This is the part of the question that carries most marks — 15 marks out of the total of 40. If in all other respects the questions seem to be equally difficult or easy, you should choose the question for which you think you can write the best answer to part (e). You should follow the same advice if you have prepared for all the options, but in this case you should read all three questions carefully.

Try not to spend much more than about 5 minutes reading the questions. As there is only 1 hour available for the whole paper, too much time spent choosing a question will mean that you will have to hurry at least one of your answers, probably the answer to part (e), which is the most important part of the question.

Examinable skills

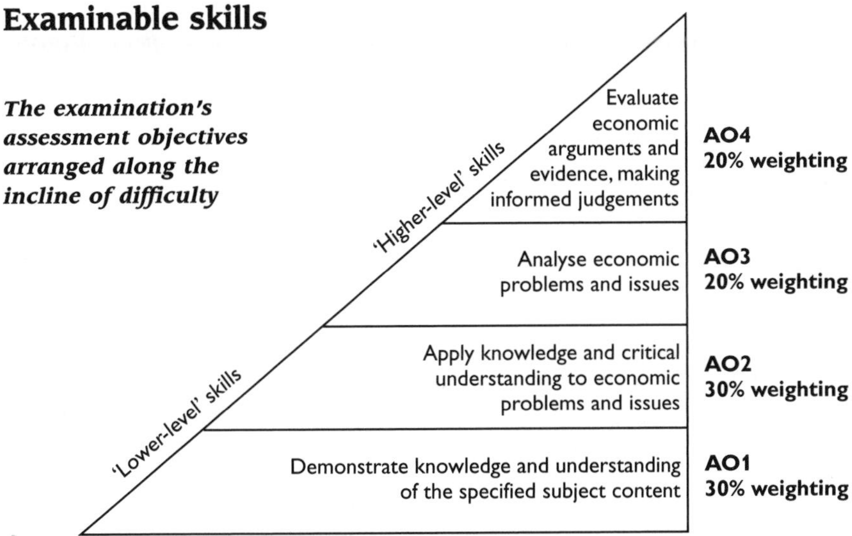

The examination has four **assessment objectives** (AOs), together with their examination weightings, arranged in an incline of difficulty. 'Lower-level' skills of knowledge and factual recall are included in AO1 (at the bottom of the incline). Moving up the incline, increasingly 'higher-level' skills feature in the AOs: application of knowledge and critical understanding (AO2); analysis of problems (AO3); and evaluation of arguments and evidence (AO4). Overall, 60% of the examination questions are knowledge-based, testing the relatively 'lower-level' skills in AOs 1 and 2. The remaining 40% of examination questions meet AOs 3 and 4.

Data-response skills

As already explained, the Unit 3: Markets at Work examination paper ECN 3 comprises three data-response questions from which you must answer one. The DRQs are numbered questions 1, 2 and 3, with each question also labelled with the appropriate option title. Thus question 1 is on the housing market, question 2 on the environment, and question 3 on the economics of sport and leisure. Each question contains five subquestions, usually listed as (a), (b), (c), (d) and (e). The mark allocation is (a) 3 marks, (b) 4 marks, (c) 8 marks, (d) 10 marks and (e) 15 marks.

The layout and structure of the questions will be similar to the nine data-response questions included in the Question and Answer section of this guide. Each question is likely to contain between one and three sets of data, usually extracted from original sources, such as newspaper or magazine articles. When three data sets are used in a question, two are likely to be passages or text, and one is likely to be numerical: for example, a line graph, a bar graph, a pie chart or a table. When all three questions contain three data sets, they will be labelled **Extracts A**, **B** and **C** for question 1, **Extracts D**, **E** and **F** for question 2, and **Extracts G**, **H** and **I** for question 3. Text or passage data will usually be extracted or adapted from original sources, with the original source indicated. Numerical data will generally be taken from original sources, but there may be exceptions: for example, supply and demand graphs created by the examiner. Each of the three data-response questions will be structured in exactly the same way and test the same assessment objectives.

The 'incline of difficulty' illustrated in Figure 1 will always be built into the DRQs, with the earlier parts of each question being the most straightforward. The first four parts of each DRQ will be marked using an **issue-based mark scheme**, which lists the marks that can be awarded for the particular issues (and associated development) that might be included in the answer.

The last part of each DRQ differs from the earlier parts in three significant ways. First, and most obviously, the last part of the question carries more marks than the earlier three parts — 37% of the total marks for the paper. If you time the examination incorrectly and fail to develop your answer to part (e) beyond a cursory footnote, you will reduce considerably your chance of achieving grade A. Second, whereas questions (a) and (b) should be answered quite briefly, you are expected to write an extended answer of several paragraphs for part (e). You should think of this as a 'mini' essay. (Questions (c) and (d), which carry 8 and 10 marks each, fall between these extremes. Their answers require some development, but not as much as part (e).) Third, 'higher-level' skills are expected for part (e). Because of this, a completely different type of mark scheme, known as a **levels of response mark scheme**, is used for the last part of each DRQ. It is vital for you to familiarise yourself with this mark scheme and to bear it in mind when you practise data-response questions.

The structure of each of the questions in the Unit 3 examination changes in the summer 2003 examination. From summer 2003, the parts of each question are likely to be:

(a) What is meant by the term...? (3 marks)
(b) Describe (an aspect of the data)... (4 marks)
(c) Explain (a feature of the data)... (8 marks)
(d) With the help of a diagram, explain why or how... (10 marks)
(e) Identify and evaluate... (15 marks)

The nine questions in the Question and Answer section of this guide generally follow this structure, for which the total mark is 40. (If you are taking the examination before summer 2003, the structure of the questions is slightly different, and the total mark is 50.)

Part (e) carries significantly more marks than parts (a) and (b) and therefore requires a longer and more developed answer. Whereas the earlier parts of the question are firmly based on defining concepts and explaining elements of the data, you should expect part (e) to 'veer away from the data'. The key instruction words are likely to be 'Identify and evaluate'. Other possibilities are 'Discuss', 'Assess' and 'Justify your reasoning'. For example:

Identify and evaluate the possible effects (either on the relevant market or on some aspect of the wider economy) of (one or more of the events described in the data).

The key command word(s) must be obeyed for your answer to reach the higher Level 4 and Level 5 standards of attainment set out in the levels of response mark scheme. Part (e) is the only part of the whole examination paper set specifically to meet AO4: evaluation of arguments and evidence, and the making of informed judgements. Your answer must evaluate the different arguments you set out. With many questions, discussion should centre on evaluating the advantages and disadvantages of, or the costs and benefits of, or the 'case for' versus the 'case against', a course of action mentioned in the question.

Finally, always try to finish your answer with a conclusion, the nature of which should vary according to the type of discussion or evaluation required. The conclusion might judge the relative strengths of the arguments discussed, possibly highlighting the most important argument. With many questions it is more appropriate to conclude whether, on balance, the 'case for' is stronger than the 'case against' and to provide some credible and reasoned justification for your opinion.

Even if your conclusion sits on the fence, saying little more than 'it all depends on circumstances', it can earn marks in two different ways. First, a conclusion that justifies your opinion provides the examiner marking your script with evidence of evaluation — the skill needed for your answer to reach a Level 5 standard. Second, the mark band descriptors used for assessing part (e) incorporate statements that relate to the quality of written communication in your answer. To earn maximum marks for this, your answer must be well organised and this requires a suitable conclusion.

A strategy for tackling the examination

This strategy assumes that you have prepared for at least two of the three options. If you have prepared a single option, ignore points 1–3.

(1) On opening the examination booklet, spend up to 5 minutes reading all three questions (if you have prepared for all the options) or the two relevant questions (if you have prepared for two of the options).
(2) Skim read through the data in each question, but read more carefully all the parts of the questions, paying special attention to part (e) in each case.
(3) Carefully select the question that you think you can answer best.
(4) Assuming you have 55 minutes to answer your chosen question, write the following time allocations in the margin against each part of the question: part (a) 4 minutes; part (b) 5 minutes; part (c) 10 minutes; part (d) 13 minutes; part (e) 23 minutes.
(5) Answer all parts of the question, preferably in the correct order, sticking rigidly to the time allocation. The time allocation, which uses up all the available time, can be shortened slightly to allow yourself up to 5 minutes to read through all your answers when you have completed all parts to the question. Don't over-develop any of your answers to the early parts of the question, but remember also that a single-sentence answer seldom answers the question properly.
(6) Clearly label each of your answers with the correct letter ((a), (b), (c), etc.), as nothing annoys an examiner more than a script in which all the answers are jumbled up together.
(7) Don't waste time copying out the questions, but leave a few lines at the end of each part of your answer in case you have time at the end to add an extra sentence or two.
(8) For each part of the question, think vary carefully about what it requires you to do, and make sure you *obey* the key instruction word.
(9) You probably haven't got time to write plans for each part of the question, except part (e) where a short plan might help you to write a better answer.

Revision planning

The revision strategy you should devise for Unit 3: Markets at Work is rather different from the strategy appropriate for Unit 1: Markets and Market Failure and Unit 2: The National Economy. There are two reasons for this. First, and most important, the specification (or syllabus) for Unit 3 does not require you to learn any concepts, terms or theories over and above those you should already have learnt when preparing for the Unit 2 and Unit 3 examinations. The specification advises that: 'Provided candidates have developed a sound grasp of the economic principles specified in Markets and Market Failure and The National Economy, the information contained in the data provided in the Markets at Work questions should be enough to answer all parts of the question on the candidate's chosen option.'

Second, the Unit 3 examination takes place several days after the Units 1 and 2 examinations, both of which take place in a morning or afternoon session on the same day. In the weeks before the 3-week 'examination season', you should revise exclusively for Markets and Market Failure and The National Economy, giving little or no thought to Markets at Work, except in so far as you are still completing your course of learning. During the year, your teacher should have followed this advice provided by the specification: 'During their course of study, candidates should be given the opportunity to answer questions on their chosen Markets at Work optional topic and to become familiar with the context of the topic.' This means your teacher should have taught you about the housing market and/or the environment and/or the economics of sport and leisure, particularly towards the end of the course, and given you a number of practice questions taken from past examination questions or possibly from this guide.

The Content Guidance section of this guide provides a summary of the information you are advised to know about all three optional topics. You should familiarise yourself with the information set out in this guide which is appropriate for your chosen topic or topics. Do this preferably during the latter stages of your taught course, say from March to May before the summer examination, and certainly in the few days in which you will be revising exclusively for the Unit 3 examination, having already sat the exams for Units 1 and 2.

The revision strategy below is based on the use of this guide, supplemented by other resources such as the notes you have built up over your course of study and favoured textbooks. The programme is designed for a period of about a week between the exams on Units 1 and 2 and the Markets at Work examination. The strategy assumes you are revising at least one other AS subject during the same week, but are able to devote a session of 2 hours (plus half an hour for short breaks) to economics every day. The strategy can be modified to meet your personal needs and preferences: for example, by shortening each revision session and/or extending the sessions over a revision period longer than a week. The strategy might also have to be modified if you are preparing for more than one option. In this case, if you decide to revise all the appropriate topics, you will have to extend the amount of timed devoted to revision. Alternatively, you may decide to revise some but not all of the topics included in this guide.

Note: You are strongly advised to use the Student Unit Guides for Units 1 and 2, which are also published by Philip Allan Updates, when revising for Markets and Market Failure and The National Economy in the weeks before you start revising for Markets at Work. The strategy set out below assumes that you have already revised for Units 1 and 2, preferably using the Philip Allan Updates Student Unit Guides.

(1) Revise one topic from the Content Guidance section of this guide per revision session. Divide the revision session into four half-hour periods during which you are working solidly and without distraction, interspersed with 10-minute breaks.
(2) Proceed through the topics in the order they appear in the guide, selecting only those that are appropriate for your chosen option or options.

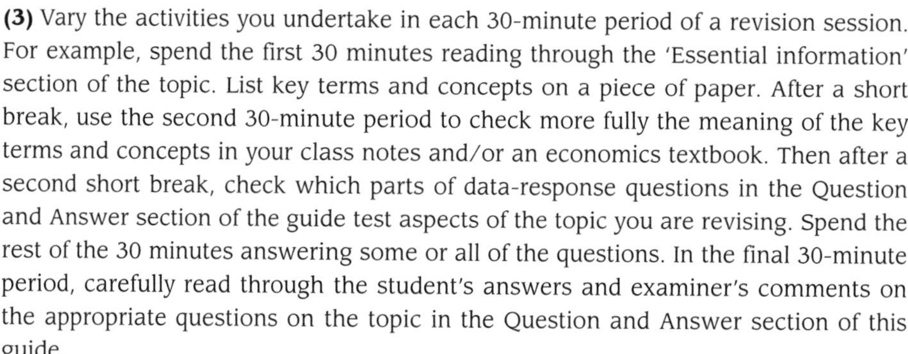

(3) Vary the activities you undertake in each 30-minute period of a revision session. For example, spend the first 30 minutes reading through the 'Essential information' section of the topic. List key terms and concepts on a piece of paper. After a short break, use the second 30-minute period to check more fully the meaning of the key terms and concepts in your class notes and/or an economics textbook. Then after a second short break, check which parts of data-response questions in the Question and Answer section of the guide test aspects of the topic you are revising. Spend the rest of the 30 minutes answering some or all of the questions. In the final 30-minute period, carefully read through the student's answers and examiner's comments on the appropriate questions on the topic in the Question and Answer section of this guide.

(4) Answer questions from past AQA examination papers and from AQA's 'Specimen Units and Mark Schemes' booklet, which your teacher should have. Make sure your teacher obtains all the relevant AQA past exam papers that are available at the time you take the examination. Identify and then answer questions from past papers that relate to the topic just revised. Then check your answer(s) against the AQA mark scheme(s) to see how you could improve.

(5) To vary your revision programme, and to make sure you reinforce and retain the vital information you have revised, try and fit some of the activities suggested below into 10-minute follow-up sessions — whenever you find yourself with a few spare minutes:

- **Write definitions** of some key terms and concepts relating to the topic revised on the previous day. Check each of your definitions against the correct definition in this guide, in a textbook or in your class notes.
- **Draw key diagrams** relating to the topic. Check any diagram you draw against a correct version of the diagram, making absolutely sure that the diagram is correctly and clearly labelled.
- Whenever you make mistakes, **repeat these exercises** the next day or a few hours later, until you have eliminated all the mistakes.

Note: If you wish to buy your own copies of past examination papers and mark schemes contact: The Publications Department, the Assessment and Qualifications Alliance, Aldon House, 39 Heald Grove, Manchester M14 4NA (tel: 0161 953 1170).

Content Guidance

Many students believe that to do well in the Unit 3 examination, a mass of extra knowledge is needed, over and above that required for the Unit 1 and Unit 2 examinations. AQA emphasises that this is *not* the case. Indeed, you might very well harm your chance of a high grade in all three exams if you spent too long cluttering your mind with too much factual knowledge about the options. Nevertheless, it is important during your course of study, and particularly in the 2 or 3 months before the summer exams, for you to practise applying the content of the Module 1 and Module 2 specifications to at least one of the Module 3 options: the housing market; the environment; or the economics of sport and leisure.

This section of the guide provides a summary of the information most likely to appear in the data of a Unit 3 examination question, together with some advice on applying the terms, concepts, economic models and theories learnt when preparing for the Unit 1 and Unit 2 exams.

The **Introduction to the specification** (on the next page) contains a summary of the main elements of the AQA specifications for Module 1: Markets and Market Failure and Module 2: The National Economy that are most likely to feature in the Unit 3 examination. This is followed by more detail about each of the three options in the specification under the following topic headings.

You should use the Content Guidance section selectively, avoiding the temptation to stray beyond the option or options chosen by your teacher for you to study. Also, as you read through the topics relevant to your chosen option(s), you might find it useful to switch frequently between the second and third sections of this guide. The latter provides sample questions and answers together with examiner's advice.

Introduction to the specification

The AQA specification for Module 3: Markets at Work contains three sections.

12.1 The housing market

The AQA specification (or syllabus) states that the market for housing includes the **owner-occupied sector**, **private rented accommodation**, **housing associations** and **local authority housing**. The specification lists a number of ways in which you may be required to apply your knowledge and understanding of concepts, principles and economic models learnt in Modules 1 and 2. These are:

- using the model of price determination in competitive markets to analyse the reasons for regional differences in house prices
- interpreting data and using economic concepts and principles to explain changes in the pattern of housing tenure
- considering evidence for market failure in the housing market and assessing the merits of different types of government intervention to ease the problem
- explaining relationships between the housing market and developments in the national economy

Specific topics on which questions might be set include: changes in housing tenure in the UK; factors influencing the demand and/or supply of housing; the determination of house prices and rents; housing as a merit good; regulation of the housing market (e.g. rent controls); and relationships between the housing market and other markets.

12.2 The environment

The specification advises that if you choose this option, you will be expected to appreciate the contribution that economics can make to understanding environmental issues and to solving environmental problems. You must understand how economic decisions affect the environment, the nature of environmental problems, and possible solutions involving, for example, taxation, subsidy and regulation. The contexts in which exam questions may be set include transport, industry and housing and the environment, and the impact of economic growth on the environment. Some of the ways in which you may be required to apply your knowledge and understanding of concepts, principles and economic models learnt in Modules 1 and 2 are:

- explaining, in the context of the material provided in the data, why environmental problems are an example of market failure
- considering the contribution that markets can make to reducing environmental problems

- analysing the role of government policies, such as indirect taxation and regulation, in reducing environmental problems
- assessing the significance of developments in the national economy for the environment

Environmental issues on which questions might be set include: types of environmental pollution and pollution as a negative externality; renewable and non-renewable resources; recycling; the problem of congestion; and economic growth and the environment.

12.3 The economics of sport and leisure

The specification states that the market for leisure is taken to include holidays and travel, the film industry, television, the theatre, the music industry and other forms of entertainment. When exam questions are set on specific leisure markets, the context in which the question is set will provide sufficient factual knowledge about the market. You are *not* expected to have a detailed knowledge of particular sports or leisure markets. Some of the ways in which you may be required to apply your knowledge and understanding of concepts, principles and economic models learnt in Modules 1 and 2 are:

- applying demand and supply analysis to help explain the prices charged for entry to watch different sporting or leisure events
- interpreting data and using economic concepts, such as income elasticity of demand, to help explain the change in the output of different sectors of the markets for leisure and sport
- assessing the significance of the development of monopoly supply in particular market sectors
- analysing the effect of interest rate and/or exchange rate changes on an industry such as the travel industry

Examples of areas where questions might be set include: the growth in the markets for sport and leisure; factors that influence the demand for sport and leisure activities; changes in the pattern of demand for sport and leisure activities; the determinants of the supply of sport and leisure activities; the environmental impact of sport and leisure activities; the impact of government policy on the industry; and the industry and the macroeconomic environment.

Terms, concepts and theories

Checklist of Unit 1 terms, concepts and theories

- the purpose of economic activity
- the economic problem, scarcity, the need for choice and opportunity cost
- economic resources and factors of production

- the possible objectives of economic agents: individuals, households, firms and the government
- conflicts between objectives and possible trade-offs
- the nature of a competitive market
- supply and demand diagrams, equilibrium, disequilibrium, excess demand and excess supply
- shifts of demand and supply curves
- elasticity: price elasticity of demand and supply, income elasticity of demand and cross elasticity of demand
- substitutes, complementary goods and derived demand
- normal goods and inferior goods
- how changes in one market can affect other markets
- the signalling, incentive and rationing (allocative) functions of prices
- monopoly and how monopoly may restrict output and raise price
- possible benefits of monopoly including economies of scale
- specialisation and the division of labour
- the meaning of production and productivity
- productive efficiency and allocative efficiency
- the meaning of market failure
- causes of market failure: monopoly, public goods, positive and negative externalities, merit goods, demerit goods, income inequalities
- government policies to make markets work better and to correct market failure: taxation, subsidy, redistribution, regulation, tradable permits to pollute, price controls and buffer stock policies
- the meaning and causes of government failure

Checklist of Unit 2 terms, concepts and theories

- the meaning of national income and output
- its measurement: GDP
- understanding data in the form of index numbers
- the distinction between nominal and real economic variables
- the objectives of a government's macroeconomic policy: full employment, growth, controlling inflation and a satisfactory balance of payments
- the main causes (types) of unemployment
- excess demand and rising costs as causes of inflation
- the role of monetary policy (interest rates) in controlling inflation
- the meaning of aggregate demand and aggregate supply
- using the AD/AS macroeconomic model to analyse economic events, the level of economic activity, and the effect of government intervention and policy
- components of aggregate demand and their effect on economic activity: consumption, investment, government spending, exports
- leakages of demand from the economy: saving, taxation and imports
- the current account of the balance of payments and the exchange rate
- fiscal policy and supply-side policies

The housing market

These notes, which relate to AQA specification section 12.1, prepare you to answer AQA examination questions on:

- the structure of housing markets
- demand and supply
- market failure and housing markets
- housing markets and the national economy

The structure of housing markets

Although the option is titled 'The Housing Market', there are in fact many housing markets in the UK. Indeed, because each house is unique in terms of **location** and **features of the property**, it has been argued that there are as many markets as there are houses: namely, over 25 million in the UK. This is probably going too far, but it does remind us that houses are seldom perfect **substitutes** for each other.

Housing tenure

Housing markets can be separated according to the type of property (flats, semi-detached and detached houses, etc.), but most importantly by the type of **tenure** enjoyed by the household living in the property. (A **household** is not the same as a **family**. For example, a family placing an elderly grandparent in sheltered accommodation creates a new one-person household. Likewise a teenager leaving the family home to live in a flat becomes a new household.) When discussing the structure of UK housing markets, four main types of tenure can be identified. Table 1 lists the main three in order of their importance in 2000, and for owner occupancy and private rental also shows how owner occupancy grew at the expense of private rented accommodation during the twentieth century. (See question 3 on page 66 for data showing details of recent changes in types of tenure.)

Housing sector	% of households in 1900	% of households in 2000
Owner occupied	10	70
Rented from local authorities	—	20
Private rental	90	10

Table 1 Changes in tenure of UK housing, 1900–2000

(1) In the **owner-occupied** sector, households own their property — though very often houses are mortgaged. A **mortgage** is a loan from a bank or building society, secured against the value of the house. When initially buying houses, very few owner-occupiers have enough money to buy outright. (Those who do are called **cash buyers**.) Most need a mortgage. For example, a **first-time buyer** may purchase a £100,000 house with a £90,000 mortgage, repayable over 25 years. If the person becomes unemployed and fails to make repayments and/or pay interest on the loan, the bank or building society may **repossess** the house, leaving the person homeless. Owner-occupiers only become outright owners of their houses once they have paid off their mortgages, usually many years after the initial purchase of the properties.

There are several *causes* of the growth of owner occupancy, such as **favourable tax treatment** and the role of **housing as a wealth asset**, which are explained below.

(2) The **local authority rented sector**, often known as **council housing** or **social housing**, consists of houses often specially built by local government and rented at a rate subsidised by taxpayers. Council houses were first built after the First World War, to try to correct **market failure** in the housing market, which had led to low-income families living for the most part in **slum** private rented accommodation. From 1979 onwards, however, UK governments, particularly Mrs Thatcher's Conservative administrations, believed that building '**ghetto**' council estates, often inhabited by very-low-income families, meant that the problem of **government failure** was more significant than that of market failure. Government policy switched to reducing rather than increasing the size of the council house sector.

(3) The **private rented sector**, where **landlords** rent the properties they own to private **tenants**, declined in the twentieth century, as Table 1 shows. Once the dominant form of housing in the UK, it now takes a relatively insignificant position. The private rented sector declined for two main reasons: the imposition of **rent controls** below the free-market level; and the granting of **security of tenure**, which prevented landlords evicting tenants. These controls were introduced to correct the alleged market failure of landlords exploiting tenants by charging excessive rents and evicting without good reason. However, by creating a shortage of private rented accommodation and **excess demand**, they further contributed to government failure in the housing market.

(4) The **housing association sector** (not shown in Table 1) comprises charities and other non-profit-making organisations known as **Registered Social Landlords (RSLs)**. These combine private and public funds to provide housing for those on low incomes. Housing associations are the smallest sector in the housing market, but through a process of new building and **transfer of housing from local authorities**, they grew rapidly from almost zero in 1981 to over a million dwellings in 2000. Housing associations now account for about 5% of housing, and this is set to increase. A high proportion of tenants (who in earlier decades would have been council tenants) are nominated by local authorities. By claiming **housing benefit**, many tenants have some or all of their rent paid by central government. RSLs are entitled to government grants to finance further house building, provided they can also raise private funding.

Regional housing markets

Newspapers often refer to the **north/south divide**, which certainly exists in the UK housing market. House prices and private rents are much higher in London and the southeast region than they are in other UK regions, though there are pockets of high-priced housing outside the southeast in locations such as the Manchester and

Leeds commuter belts and Edinburgh. By 2001, the average price of houses in Greater London had risen above £200,000 and the number of 'millionaire' properties was proliferating, while at the other extreme, run-down houses in declining and increasingly derelict northern manufacturing regions were selling for less than £5,000 — if a buyer could be found. The factors explaining differences in regional house prices include the **immobility of housing**, the **poor quality** of housing in some locations (though much badly built housing in London now commands high prices), but primarily **supply and demand factors**. Factors affecting the supply of housing in different regions include the **availability of building land** and the operation of **planning controls**. Demand factors, which relate strongly to the relative **success of regional economies**, include **population density and growth** (both of which are in turn affected by **migration** between regions), and marked regional differences in personal income and wealth, together with the lending policies of financial intermediaries.

Besides understanding the *causes* of different regional house prices, you might also be asked to discuss the *effects*. By making it difficult, if not impossible, for low-income families to move to the southeast in search of jobs, regional price differences contribute to the **immobility of labour**. (Think how the growth of owner occupancy at the expense of affordable rented accommodation contributes.) Also, workers living in the southeast may be reluctant to move to a job outside the region. Although they would be able to buy much larger houses with the money raised from the sale of their southeastern properties, they fear they could never afford to move back again.

European housing markets

High rates of owner occupancy, similar to and often higher than the UK's, occur in some other European countries, notably Finland, Greece and Spain. However, in others, such as Switzerland with an owner occupancy rate of only 40%, and Germany, rented accommodation is much more significant. By contributing to a more geographically mobile labour force, the availability of affordable rented housing has been a factor in the economic success of these countries.

Demand and supply

The markets for new and second-hand housing

New houses are mostly bought from specialist house building companies. A few large, house-building companies account for most of the new houses built in the UK. Second-hand houses are generally bought from their existing occupiers who wish to sell. With these transactions, the act of selling a house simultaneously creates a demand, in the sense that the seller needs another house to live in.

The long-run rise in the price of housing

There has been a long-run trend for house prices to rise in the UK, ignoring short-run 'booms and busts'. Both the demand for and the supply of housing have increased (or shifted rightwards) in the long run, but demand has increased faster. Supply has increased because the quantity of new houses added to the housing stock each year exceeds the number demolished or converted to other uses. The supply of housing for owner occupancy has generally increased even faster because landlords have withdrawn from the rental market and sold their properties. Sometimes, however, when housing market conditions are more favourable for private letting, the reverse happens. The main causes of the long-run rightward shift of demand have been: population growth; the growth in the number of households; real income growth (housing being a **normal good** with a positive **income elasticity of demand**); and people switching to owner occupancy, which they treat as a **superior good** (income elasticity of demand > +1) and away from the perceived **inferior substitute** — rented accommodation.

Short-run fluctuations in the price of housing

These fluctuations are explained primarily by the short-run demand curve shifting rightwards or leftwards along the near-vertical short-run supply curve. Figure 1 shows the demand curve shifting rightwards from D_1 to D_2, causing house prices to rise from P_1 to P_2, with only a small increase in supply.

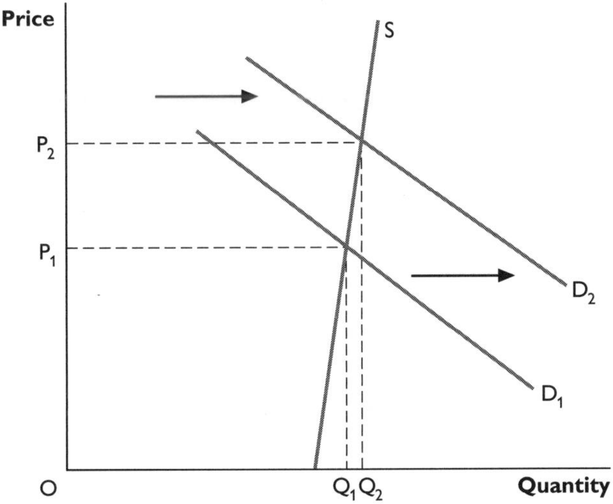

Figure 1 Short-term changes in the price of housing

The short-run supply of housing

In the short run, as Figure 1 shows, the supply of housing is highly **price inelastic** or **unresponsive to price changes**. The factors that explain this include: the general shortage of land; the effect of planning controls, which make it difficult to convert land from other uses; and the length of time taken to build a new house.

The demand for housing

As with all **consumer goods**, people demand housing for the **utility** or **welfare** derived from the **consumer services** that houses provide. All houses provide basic **shelter**, but each and every house also has a particular combination of other consumer

attributes, such as location, a view, a garden, car parking and rooms suitable for work, leisure and hospitality. However, the demand for housing is also affected by a number of special factors. Housing is a **consumer durable good**, delivering a stream of consumer services over a very long period, often a century or more. Unlike most durable goods, such as cars and television sets, which depreciate and lose value during their lives, most houses — or certainly the land on which they are built — **appreciate** and gain value. This means that the demand for housing is determined not only by people's need for shelter, but by the fact that people treat housing as a form of **investment**. Housing is an attractive **wealth asset** — indeed, the main wealth asset owned by many UK residents.

As a result, far from reducing demand, a rise in house prices can trigger a speculative bubble in the house market in which rising prices drive up demand, causing a further rise in prices, with the process continuing until the bubble bursts. Rising house prices mean that owner-occupiers already on the 'housing ladder' have a vested interest in further price rises. Existing owner-occupiers become wealthier because the value of their property rises but the value of their mortgages generally stays the same. They benefit from **capital gains** — the difference between the price paid for the house and its current higher market value. In this situation, there is an increase in the number of 'first-time buyers', as young people, desperate to get on the 'housing ladder', try to buy houses before they become unaffordable. Moreover, wishing to become even more wealthy, existing owner-occupiers put their houses on the market and '**trade up**' to buy larger properties or houses in more desirable locations. Both these events shift the demand curve for housing rightwards and fuel a further rise in house prices. During house market booms, activity in the housing market soars with increases in both the number of people trying to sell and the number trying to buy property. However, demand rises faster than supply.

Market failure and housing

The causes of market failure in UK housing markets

Free-market forces operated in UK housing markets in the nineteenth century and before the First World War. But the way the housing market operated meant, first, that most of the population could not afford to buy a house at the price established by the market and, second, that many people renting property lived in very poor-quality slum accommodation. Some economists considered these to be market failures in the housing market, though it could also be argued that they were problems of poverty and unequal income distribution rather than housing market failures *per se*.

For much of the twentieth century, UK governments were concerned with the second of these two alleged market failures: exploitation of tenants by landlords. Good-quality housing can be regarded as a **merit good** possessing two characteristics:

- The **social benefits** for the whole community resulting from a family being well housed are greater than the **private benefits** enjoyed by the family.

- The **long-term private benefits** enjoyed by the family — for example, in terms of longer life expectancy and good health — are greater than the **short-term private benefits**.

Methods of government intervention in housing markets

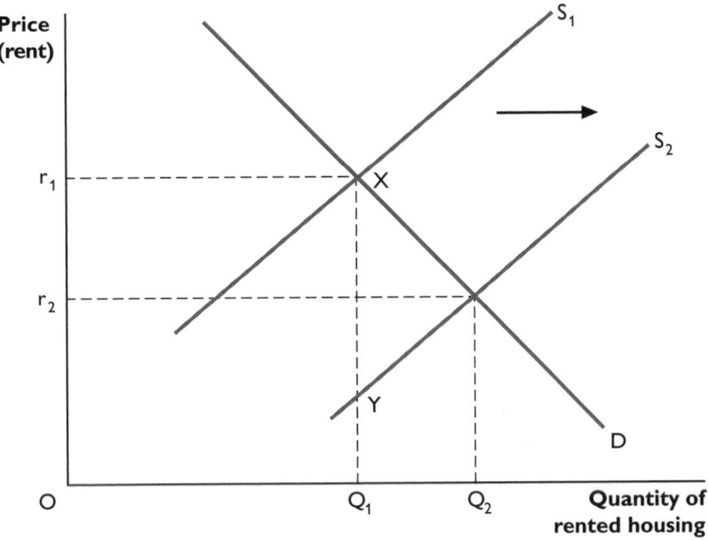

Figure 2 The effect of subsidising rents in the market for rented accommodation

If decent-quality housing is a merit good, the free market leads to an outcome in which house prices and rents are too high. Too few people, particularly among the poor, end up living in houses of adequate quality. There is therefore a case for government intervention to bring down the price of housing, and in particular to make sure that affordable rented accommodation of decent quality is available for the poor. (It can also be argued that poor-quality slum housing is a **demerit good** and that governments should implement policies to discourage its consumption.)

Figure 2 shows how the government could use **subsidies** to reduce rents. In the absence of a subsidy, the free-market rent is r_1, and Q_1 properties are rented. But if the government pays a subsidy to the property owner equal to the vertical distance XY, the supply curve of rented housing shifts rightwards to S_2. The subsidised rent now falls to r_2 and the quantity of rentals increases to Q_2.

Rents have been subsidised in the UK, but for the most part, socially provided rented property (council houses) rather than private rentals have been subsidised. In recent years there has been a shift away from subsidy towards providing **housing benefit** to low-income families to enable them to pay market rents.

Government failure in housing markets

To be effective in correcting market failure in the housing market, government intervention must make more accommodation available, especially for poor families, than would be the case in an unregulated free market. Council house building by local authorities should have this effect, though the **opportunity cost** could include the effect of higher taxes elsewhere in the economy and diversion of resources from other uses. If government intervention is ineffective or if, more seriously, it not only fails to correct market failure but makes matters worse, problems of **government failure** result. The rapid deterioration of many council estates into 'sink' ghettos, in which nobody wants to live, provides an example. Because of this problem, recent UK governments have tried to switch much of the stock of social housing into ownership by housing associations, believing that private charitable owners stand a better chance of maintaining the quality of the housing stock and the quality of tenants' lives.

Another example of well-intentioned government intervention in the housing market sometimes making matters worse rather than better is provided by the history of **rent controls** in the private rented sector in the mid-twentieth century. The effect of rent controls is illustrated in Figure 3.

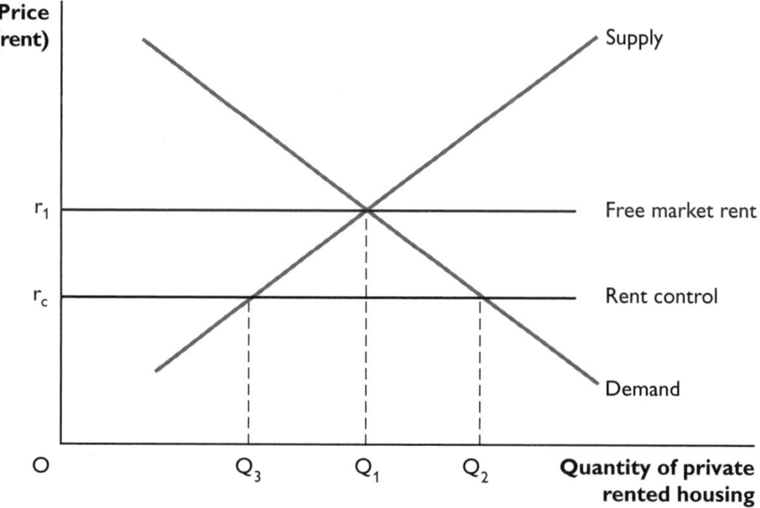

Figure 3 The effect of rent controls

Having decided on the ground of **inequity** (unfairness) that the free market rent r_1 was excessive, the UK government imposed a maximum rent or **price ceiling** at r_c. Landlords responded by reducing from Q_1 to Q_3 the quantity of houses they were willing to let. At the same time, the low controlled rent increased demand among prospective tenants to Q_2. **Excess demand**, or a shortage of rented housing, equal to Q_2 minus Q_3 resulted.

Landlords found that their ability to remove rented accommodation from the market depended on whether they could evict **sitting tenants**. In the 1960s, UK governments introduced new laws that made it almost impossible to evict a tenant legally, against the tenant's will. This led to (1) criminal activity by rogue landlords, using violence to 'persuade' tenants to leave, (2) property being switched from private letting as soon as tenants died or could be evicted and (3) almost no new properties being built for private rental. Thus government intervention to correct a perceived market failure became the main factor creating the shortage of private rented accommodation. The shortage still persists today, despite legislation in the 1980s and 1990s to remove rent controls and to make it easier for landlords to evict tenants.

Other examples of market failure and government failure in the UK housing market

The UK has one of the highest population densities in Europe, particularly in the southeast. In the 1930s, free-market forces uninhibited by any **planning controls** led to **ribbon development** along the main roads extending out of towns and cities, and the **conurbanisation** of much previously agricultural land around large cities, particularly London. To prevent the whole of the southeast becoming a continuous built-up area, **green belts** and other limitations to house building were introduced. Most economists believe that these and other planning controls were necessary and have been successful. However, by severely restricting the amount of land available for building new houses, planning controls have been an important cause of high and often unaffordable house prices in the southeast. Planning controls have also made it difficult to switch land between different uses to meet new circumstances.

Recent UK governments have regarded owner occupancy as even more of a merit good than housing in general. Conservative politicians favour owner occupancy because they believe it influences voting behaviour in their direction, while 'New' Labour has become almost as committed to owner occupancy. Governments have therefore used fiscal policy and the tax system to encourage owner occupancy. Although owner occupancy has many virtues, such as creating incentives for households to improve their properties, at the macro level, if taken to excess, it contributes to three significant problems:

- Geographical immobility of labour harms the supply side of the economy and national economic performance.
- Housing enjoys tax advantages not given to investment in industry. Arguably, too high a proportion of household savings has been diverted into the property market and away from company finance.
- UK households have much larger mortgage debt than households in other European countries and this adversely affects UK monetary policy. Changes in interest rates have a disproportionate effect on households' consumption and saving, and this destabilises aggregate demand and the national economy.

Housing markets and the national economy

We can use the **aggregate demand/aggregate supply (AD/AS)** macroeconomic model shown in Figure 4 to explain some of the ways in which UK housing markets affect the national economy.

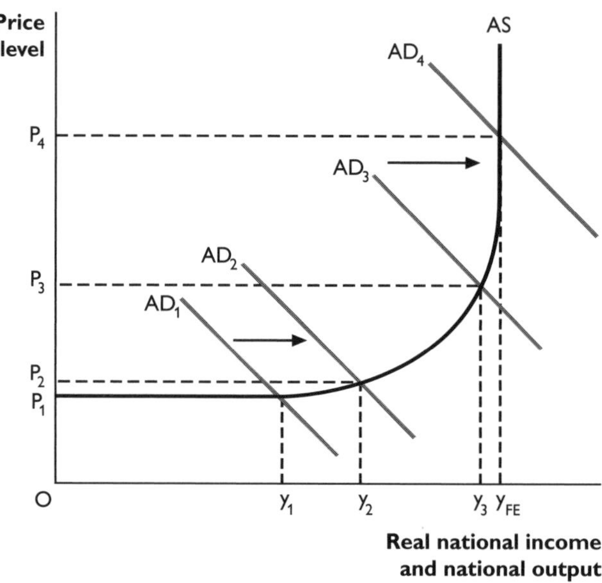

Figure 4 The AD/AS model and the housing market

Economic activity in the housing market tends to affect **aggregate demand** more than **aggregate supply**. **Consumption spending** is the largest component of aggregate demand and, in turn, spending on housing is one of the largest components of consumption, particularly if we include spending on **complementary goods** such as carpets, bathroom and kitchen furniture, cookers and washing machines.

Suppose the AD curve is initially in the position AD_1. This means that the economy is in **recession**, suffering from **deficient aggregate demand**, since the level of output y_1 is well below the full employment level of output y_{FE}. The AD curve must shift rightwards to bring about **economic recovery** and end the recession. In the UK, spending on housing and other consumer goods has generally led recovery from recession. (The 1990–92 recession was an exception. In this case, consumer confidence remained low and the housing market stagnated long after the recession ended. Following devaluation of the exchange rate in 1992, investment spending on capital goods and exports started the economic recovery.)

As Figure 4 shows, a consumer and housing market boom at the end of a recession has largely beneficial effects. Output rises to y_2, thereby creating jobs and reducing unemployment, but there is relatively little inflation, the price level only rising from P_1 to P_2. Problems arise, however, when spending on housing increases as the economy approaches full employment. The AD curve shifts rightwards, for example from AD_3 to AD_4, but because of insufficient spare capacity in the economy, **excess demand** pulls up the price level from P_3 to P_4 in a **demand-pull** inflation.

Because of the importance of owner-occupied housing in the UK, 'boom and bust' in the housing market tends to promote and exacerbate 'boom and bust' in the whole economy, i.e. it makes the **business cycle** more volatile. Owner-occupiers (but not tenants) benefit tremendously from rising house prices. They enjoy tax-free capital gains and become much wealthier. Consumption is positively related to personal **wealth** as well as to **income**. This means that when households become wealthier, consumption rises at all levels of income, and saving falls. In effect, when house prices are rising rapidly, owner-occupiers don't need to save to increase their wealth because **house price inflation** is doing the job for them. Consumption is also positively related to **consumer confidence**. Rising house prices usually give rise to increased consumer confidence and a '**feel-good factor**', further boosting consumption.

Towards the peak of economic booms, house prices have risen much faster than inflation in general. At this point, **monetary policy** has been used to try to reduce house price inflation and the consumer spending spree it generates. However, excessive house price inflation has generally been restricted to the more prosperous parts of the UK where **service industries** rather than **manufacturing** are the mainstay of the economy. Raising **interest rates** to control house price inflation in London and the southeast has the unfortunate effect of reducing aggregate demand in all regions, thus throwing manufacturing regions, if not the whole economy, into recession. This is the problem of '**two-speed Britain**'. Regions dependent on manufacturing require low interest rates to nurture their fragile economies, but their needs are overridden by high interest rates targeted at the overheated property market in the southeast of England.

Housing markets and aggregate supply

Although housing markets affect the national economy primarily through their effect on aggregate demand, they also affect aggregate supply. Aggregate supply, economic growth and national competitiveness may have been adversely affected over the years by: (1) the prevalence of owner occupation and the lack of private rented accommodation at affordable rents, contributing to the geographical immobility of labour and labour market rigidity; and (2) the favourable tax treatment granted to housing, diverting savings out of productive investment in industry. The economy's long-run AS curve may have shifted rightwards at a slower rate than would have been the case without these adverse effects.

How the national economy affects housing markets

Not only do housing markets affect the economy, but also the economy in turn affects housing markets. Owner-occupied housing is a **normal good**, and indeed a **superior good**, with an **income elasticity of demand** greater than +1. This means that **economic growth** in the whole economy leads to a larger proportionate increase in demand for owner-occupied housing, together with all the **complementary goods** that go with housing. And as we have just seen, monetary policy (interest rate changes) affects housing markets.

Government fiscal policy also affects housing markets in significant ways. Until quite recently, people buying houses on a mortgage could claim **income tax relief**, i.e. they did not pay income tax on part of their income equal to some or all of the interest

payments on their mortgage. Although this and other tax reliefs related to housing have now been abolished, owner-occupiers still enjoy two huge tax advantages denied to tenants of rented accommodation.

When selling houses, owner-occupiers can enjoy all the **capital gain** tax-free, i.e. their houses are generally exempt from capital gains tax.

Owner-occupiers used to pay income tax on the **imputed income** yielded by their properties. This is the income they would have received from the property if they had chosen to be landlords, letting the property for gain. The abolition of this tax has meant that owner-occupiers escape tax on the benefits received from the houses they own and live in. Meanwhile, tenants have to pay income tax on the income used to pay rents, and all the benefit of any capital gain on the property goes to the landlord.

The building cycle

The level of economic activity in the national economy also affects the construction industry. Since the 1970s, the house-building industry has become increasingly dominated by a small number of 'volume' builders. The building companies buy land when the economy is in recession. The builder holds the land in a 'land bank' until the economy recovers. Houses are then built in the expectation of being sold during or shortly after construction. The process tends to be speculative — very few houses are built to meet customers' specific requirements. The construction process itself is sometimes contracted out to smaller builders, who depend on hired plant and equipment and who mainly employ casual labour. In recessions, there is often a high level of bankruptcy among smaller building firms and subcontractors, and unemployment among building workers soars.

Positive and negative equity

The word **equity** has two very different meanings in economics. In many contexts it means **fairness** or **justness**, but its second meaning is **wealth**. People enjoy **positive equity** when the value of their **assets** (the things they own) exceeds the value of their **liabilities** (their **debts** or what they owe). During house market booms, when house price inflation runs ahead of the general rate of inflation, owner-occupiers' positive equity increases. The value of houses rises in **real** as well as **nominal** terms, and at the same time owner-occupiers benefit from the fact that their mortgage debt does not rise. In these circumstances, many owner-occupiers indulge in **equity withdrawal** or **equity leakage**. This occurs when households remortgage their properties (i.e. borrow more money secured against the now higher value of their properties), and then spend the sums borrowed on general consumption — new cars, holidays, home improvements, etc. Alternatively, many households borrow more money and increase their mortgages in order to 'trade up' to larger, more expensive properties.

Don't confuse equity withdrawal (which occurs during housing market booms) with the **negative equity trap**, which can occur in the subsequent 'bust'. This affects owner-occupiers — usually first-time buyers — who bought houses with the aid of very large mortgages at the peak of the house price boom. The fall in house prices in the late 1980s and early 1990s caused over 1 million households to suffer from negative equity — the value of their property being less than their mortgage debt. They were trapped because they did not have any equity to be able to move to another property, and their negative wealth acted to reduce their consumption. For some, the loss of employment led them to get into arrears on payment of their mortgages. In cases where they failed to gain another job, the bank or building society repossessed their properties and they were made homeless. (The sale of these repossessed properties further depressed house prices.)

Examination skills

The skills most likely to be tested by a question on the housing market are as follows:

- Interpreting and analysing data: showing different forms of housing tenure such as owner occupancy and rented accommodation, and changes in their relative importance.
- Understanding how, and explaining why and the extent to which, housing markets are interrelated.
- Applying economic theory to explain the causes of changes in the structure of housing markets.
- Identifying and evaluating how changes in the structure of housing markets may affect other markets and/or national economic performance.
- Identifying and evaluating ways in which government policy can affect the structure of housing markets.
- Using supply and demand analysis to explain *causes* of the *long-run* increase and *short-run* changes in house prices in the UK.
- Explaining why both market failure and government failure occur in the housing market.
- Identifying and evaluating government policies such as subsidy and rent controls used to correct market failure.
- Explaining how changes in housing markets affect aggregate demand and/or aggregate supply.
- Explaining how changes in the national economy, particularly those relating to the business cycle, may affect housing markets.
- Explaining how monetary policy, fiscal policy, regulations and planning controls affect housing markets.

Common examination errors

- Inability to distinguish between absolute and relative (proportionate or percentage) changes in the importance of different forms of housing.
- Confusing *causes* of changes in the structure of housing markets with *effects* of changes.
- Failure to distinguish between *long-run* and *short-run* determinants of the demand for, and the supply of, housing.
- Inability to apply the expected technical terminology of supply and demand analysis such as elasticity, equilibrium and disequilibrium, excess demand and excess supply.

- Confusion of *causes* of changes in supply and demand with the *effects* of changes.
- Failure to recognise market failure in the housing market, and the fact that there are a number of different market failures in the housing market.
- Assuming that because social housing is provided by the government, it is a *public good* rather than a *merit good*.
- Confusion of nominal house price inflation and real house price inflation.
- Confusion of equity withdrawal and negative equity.
- Failure to understand how spending on housing affects consumption and investment.

The environment

These notes, which relate to AQA specification section 12.2, prepare you to answer AQA examination questions on:

- industry and the environment
- consumers and the environment
- transport and the environment
- the national economy and the environment

Industry and the environment

Resource depletion and resource degradation

By producing consumer goods and services that people want and need, production enables **economic welfare** and human happiness to increase. Primary production uses **natural resources** provided by the environment, such as coal, oil, metals and the fertility of the soil. If carefully used and conserved, resources such as soil fertility and fish stocks can be **renewed**. However, others, such as **fossil fuels**, are **non-renewable resources**. Literally, they are 'used up' as they are used, and cannot be replaced. This is called **resource depletion**. Between these extremes, resources such as iron and copper are non-renewable in the sense that mining reduces the total quantity of the natural resource available to be extracted in the future, but renewable in so far as **recycling** is possible.

Production of goods and services also leads to **resource degradation**. This occurs when firms (and consumers) treat the atmosphere, oceans, land, rivers and lakes as a giant waste bin in which to dump the unwanted by-products of economic activity. Depletion captures the effect of activities such as logging and mining; degradation describes the **pollution** of air, water and land. Developed countries use up far more of the world's non-renewable resources than developing countries. They also contribute more to the pollution that causes global warming.

Sustainable and unsustainable economic activity

Some economists believe that resource depletion and degradation will eventually make economic growth **unsustainable**, at least for most of the world's population.

They believe that: (1) the world's non-renewable natural resources will be exhausted; (2) the world's pollution problem will become so acute that the capacity for self-cleaning and regeneration will be exhausted; and (3) as population continues to grow, it will reach a point where mankind will destroy itself through sheer weight of numbers. Free-market economists are much more optimistic. With regard to the world running out of resources, they argue that, other things being equal, an increase in the rate of resource usage will cause resource prices to rise. In their turn, rising resource prices create incentives for consumers and producers to alter their economic behaviour. Consumers economise in their purchases of goods and services. Producers, meanwhile, respond to the changing relative prices of their inputs or factors of production both by altering methods of production and by exploring the earth's crust for new supplies of minerals and fossil fuels that would be uneconomic to search for and extract at a lower resource price.

Most economists nevertheless agree on the need for sustainable economic growth and economic development. According to Professor David Pearce, **sustainable economic development** 'ensures that the needs of the present are met without compromising the ability of future generations to meet their own needs'. This does not mean 'no growth'; rather it recognises the limits of growth and looks for alternative ways of growing. Sustainable development probably requires a shift in the balance of the way economic progress is pursued. It means a change in consumption patterns towards environmentally more benign products, and a change in investment patterns towards augmenting environmental capital.

The problem of negative externalities or external costs

One of the most basic assumptions of economic theory is that firms and consumers always try to **maximise their private benefit or self-interest** (for firms this is **profit**), irrespective of the effect this has on others. But in doing so they may produce **negative externalities**, such as pollution, which **reduce social welfare** and harm the wider community — often in countries other than the country where the externality originates. An externality is a **spin-off effect** of an economic activity such as production, which affects other people known as **third parties**. Externalities are produced and received 'outside the market'. For example, people breathing polluted air are unable to charge the polluter for the '**bad**' they are unwillingly 'consuming'. The market fails because firms dump pollution on unwilling **free-riders**, without the polluter having to pay the costs of pollution. As a result, the market prices of goods such as electricity end up being too low because part of the true cost of production, the cost of pollution dumped in the environment, is not included in the price charged.

Acid rain pollution discharged by fossil-fuel-burning power stations degrades the environment by acidifying the soil, lakes and rivers. Figure 5 illustrates the resulting market failure and shows how it might be corrected. In a free market, the price of electricity is P_1. But because P_1 does not include the cost of pollution dumped in the environment, electricity is too cheap. More electricity is produced and consumed than would be the case if the price charged included the cost of pollution. This is

allocatively inefficient. Scarce resources are being allocated between industries and uses in a way that fails to maximise economic welfare.

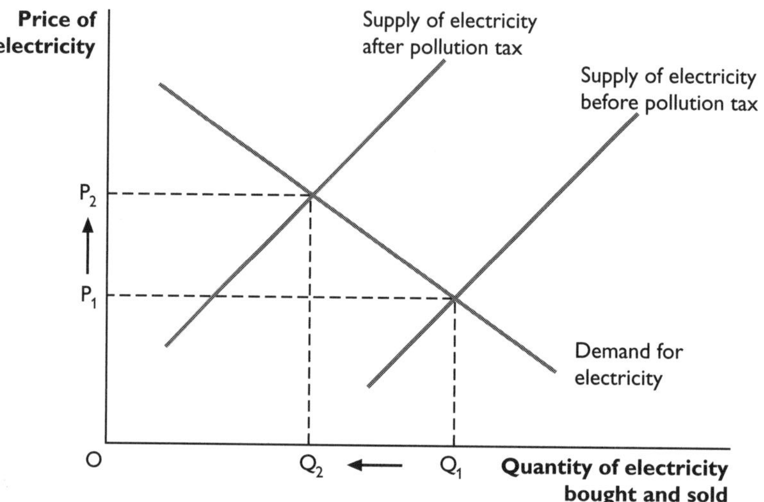

Figure 5 Electricity production and negative externalities

Government policies to correct environmental market failures

If we assume that the cost of pollution emitted by power station companies is equal to the vertical distance between the two supply curves drawn in Figure 5, the **allocatively efficient level of electricity production** is Q_2 and not the quantity the free market produces, Q_1. There are two main ways in which the government can attempt to reduce production to Q_2. These are **regulation** and **taxation**. **Banning all pollution** is the most extreme form of regulation, but this has the undesirable effect of banning the '**good**' (electricity) as well as the '**bad**' (pollution). Because this is obviously not desirable, governments usually use forms of regulation that stop short of an outright ban. Examples are **maximum emission limits**, and compulsion to use **clean fuels** and to install **clean technology**, such as filters in power station chimneys.

The second approach is to charge a **pollution tax**, based on the '**polluter must pay**' principle. The government levies a tax on the polluter equal to the estimated cost of the pollution discharged. This has an effect similar to the **incentive function of prices**. The greater the pollution, the more tax firms must pay. The tax creates an incentive for power stations to reduce pollution, in order to avoid paying the tax. The effect of a pollution tax is illustrated in Figure 5. A tax imposed on producers shifts the supply curve upwards or leftwards, thereby increasing the price of electricity to P_2. Production and consumption fall to Q_2. The tax '**internalises the externality**'. The power station company now has to cover all its costs of production, including the cost of pollution, and this is reflected in the price charged to consumers.

Besides regulation and taxation, the government might establish (1) the **private property right** to clean air and (2) a **market in permits to pollute**. The former gives people the legal right to enjoy clean air. When pollution breaches this right, the victim can use the civil law to sue the polluter for financial compensation. Permits to pollute are a mixture of regulation and 'working with the market'. The government imposes a maximum pollution emission limit, and then power stations either: (1) **exactly comply** with the emission limit; or (2) **over-comply** by reducing pollution by more than the law requires; or (3) **under-comply** by reducing pollution by less than the law requires. With simple 'command and control' regulation, the latter would break the law and be punished, usually with fines. However, with tradable permits to pollute, over-complying power stations sell their 'spare' pollution permits to under-complying power stations, enabling the latter to continue to pollute legally. Under-complying power stations are likely to use old technology or dirty fuels, which make it difficult to meet emission limits. As with a pollution tax, tradable permits to pollute 'work with the market' in that they mimic the incentive function of prices. Power stations have an incentive to over-comply because they can make money out of selling spare pollution permits. Under-complying power stations have a different incentive, namely to clean up their act to avoid incurring the higher production costs brought about by having to purchase pollution permits.

Consumers and the environment

Through profligate and wasteful behaviour, consumers add to the environmental problems resulting from production.

Environmental problems arise partly due to population growth, which obviously creates more consumers. But population growth probably contributes less to resource depletion and degradation than income growth. Very poor people scratching a living from the earth's crust are seldom much concerned with the environmental effect of their activities, such as cutting down trees to provide fuel. However, it is richer people in high-income countries, particularly the USA, who are most responsible for environmentally destructive consumer behaviour. Per head they use up far more fuel, timber products and other resources than the inhabitants of poorer countries such as India and China. Nevertheless, as incomes grow in the developing world, Third World citizens naturally tend to copy the wasteful consumer behaviour of richer countries, thereby making global environmental problems worse.

Economics teaches that, other things being equal, consumers prefer to buy cheaper rather than more expensive goods. Faced, for example, with a choice between two apparently identical tables, it makes sense to choose the one with the lowest price tag. But consider how the two tables were made. Suppose the expensive table has been made from timber cut from forests where conservation practices are followed, but the cheaper table is the product of tropical rain forest destruction. Why, in these circumstances, do many consumers still decide to buy the cheaper table? The answer lies partly in a lack of sufficient information about the origins of goods and how they are made. But even with this information, many consumers will buy the cheaper table. Consumers are prone to short-termism, tending to go for the short-term bargain even when they know it is in their long-term interest to buy

goods made in an environmentally responsible way. And while gaining all the benefit that low prices provide, individual consumers suffer little of the environmental harm. The effects of resource depletion and degradation are spread far and wide, possibly across the whole world, with future rather than today's generations suffering most of the consequences.

Consumer behaviour and externalities

In their everyday behaviour, consumers are responsible for **negative externalities** that harm the environment. These include **noise pollution** (e.g. loud music and noisy neighbours), **visual pollution** (e.g. ugly houses) and the **dumping of waste**. Externalities can range from the relatively trivial (e.g. the problem of litter) to the potentially very serious (e.g. the problem of global warming, for which the use of private motor cars and air travel is arguably the most significant single cause). As with industrial pollution, the government can use **regulation** and/or **taxation** to reduce the production of environmentally harmful consumption externalities. Governments also try to persuade people to alter behaviour and to adopt more environmentally friendly ways of life: for example, by walking and cycling, and by improving the energy efficiency of houses. Because persuasion on its own is generally ineffective, financial inducement may be necessary to alter lifestyles, such as **subsidising** public transport and solar power, while taxing private motor cars and fossil fuels.

Consumers (as well as firms) also produce **positive externalities** (or **external benefits**) that improve and conserve the environment. Tree planting is a good example. People plant trees in their gardens to gain **private benefits** such as shade and beauty. However, tree planting generates positive externalities that add to the **social benefit** of the whole community, including people living in other countries. By absorbing carbon dioxide (CO_2) from the atmosphere, trees reduce the harmful environmental effects of pollution elsewhere and slow down the process of **global warming**. To reduce the build-up of CO_2 in the atmosphere, rich countries such as the USA which discharge large amounts of global-warming gases into the atmosphere could pay poor countries to plant forests. These would act as 'carbon sinks', soaking up the CO_2 emitted by the richer countries. Large-scale tree planting could create other external benefits, such as improving water retention in the soil and reducing the flooding that follows periods of heavy rain.

Household waste and the environment

High incomes lead to high levels of consumption, which in turn lead to large amounts of waste. In much of the developed world, local government provides a rubbish collection service, often supplied free but paid for by local taxes. But when rubbish collection is free, there is no incentive to economise in its production, and people produce too much rubbish. The obvious economic solution is to charge a price for waste disposal. This creates an incentive to throw out less and **recycle** more. But charging for rubbish collection can create new environmental problems. To avoid the charge, some households may '**free-ride**' by dumping rubbish in a neighbour's bin or in a public place such as a park, thereby harming the local environment.

An example of this problem occurred recently in the UK, where much rubbish, both household and industrial, is dumped in landfill sites. These sites are rapidly filling up, so soon the UK will face the problem of what to do with rubbish. Landfill also poses problems for future generations, because pollutants can seep into ground water or enter the atmosphere. The British government therefore decided to tax the use of official landfill sites. Unfortunately, this led to practices such as 'fly-tipping' rubbish on farm land and quiet rural roads. Similarly, motorists have harmed the environment by dumping old cars in city streets. This illustrates the **law of unintended consequences**. Governments introduce regulations or taxes in order to improve the environment and to correct an alleged market failure. However, government intervention triggers consequences that the policy-makers have not foreseen, which, if sufficiently adverse, can render the policy ineffective. In extreme cases, it is argued, the resulting problems of **government failure** are worse than the market failure problem that the government is trying to correct.

Recycling

Incineration or burning rubbish is an alternative to landfill. By producing electricity, waste incineration marginally reduces the use of fossil fuels, but it also pollutes the atmosphere, not least through the emission of harmful dioxin chemicals. **Recycling waste** is a more environmentally sustainable option. Firms want to be seen as 'green' and 'environmentally friendly'. Sometimes this is little more than a cynical marketing exercise, but many firms now use recycled raw materials such as glass and paper. Automobile companies such as BMW are now building cars with a high percentage of recyclable parts. Governments promote recycling by providing facilities such as bottle banks and by requiring manufacturers to make their products recyclable. In the future, manufacturers may be required by law to take back goods such as cars and television sets once these goods have reached the end of their economic lives. Sometimes, however, recycling produces new problems. In the 1990s, German households recycled paper so enthusiastically that the market collapsed and recycling companies went out of business. For a time, paper banks went unemptied and Germans could not recycle their books and newspapers.

Shopping and the environment

Sixty years ago few people had cars or refrigerators, and household freezers had not been invented. In the UK, most households shopped daily for food and groceries at local shops in town centres and villages, or in parades of small shops in the newly built suburbs that had sprung up around larger towns and cities. Shoppers travelled by public transport, usually bus or tram, or walked. Much food, particularly vegetables and meat, was bought by local shops from local farmers. For most people, shopping was not the 'leisure activity' it often is today; incomes were lower and mostly spent on essentials.

It goes without saying that the modern pattern of shopping is completely different, though there have been attempts to revive local shops in town centres and villages to prevent the decline of local environments. Modern shopping is dominated by large retail chains, often owned by multinational corporations. Out-of-town shopping malls have sprung up, often adjacent to green-belt land. The malls have been blamed for the decline of inner-city shopping areas and small local shops. In most towns, shopping malls and high streets alike contain rows of nearly identical shops with national and international brand names.

The change in the pattern of shopping has had a significant environmental impact, both locally and globally. Food retailing is dominated by a handful of supermarket chains whose major stores are located on the edge of towns and cities. For the most part, the supermarkets do not buy from local farmers, but through supply chains extending across the world. Shoppers drive their cars to huge out-of-town stores and retail complexes, to buy goods that have already been transported by truck or plane for hundreds or thousands of miles. Bubble packs and other methods of packaging add to the problem of household and industrial waste. Though benefiting from substantial economies of scale, the large supermarket chains have been accused of destroying the rural economy in the UK. Critics claim that supermarkets use their monopoly power to pay rock-bottom prices to British farmers, thereby driving many small farmers out of business.

So, while modern retailing undoubtedly contributes significantly to high material living standards, on the debit side it is harming the environment. The issue facing citizens and governments alike is: are the environmental costs a price worth paying for the material benefits that modern retailing delivers? And if not, is it possible to make retailing more environmentally benign: for example, by controlling out-of-town superstores and malls, and by insisting that retail chains develop inner-city brown-field sites and high streets, and that they sell locally produced food wherever possible?

Transport and the environment

As we have just noted, by increasing car use and the transport of goods over long distances, modern methods of retailing may be harming the environment. But over the last hundred years, people have benefited enormously from developments in road and air transport. In particular, private ownership of cars has been a great personal liberator, enabling ordinary people to enjoy a freedom of movement unimaginable for most of human history. However, cars, trucks and aeroplanes are some of the main modern polluters, certainly as far as atmospheric pollution is concerned. Besides contributing to resource depletion by running down the earth's stock of fossil fuels, they are responsible for emitting carbon dioxide (CO_2), the main **greenhouse gas** causing **global warming**, into the atmosphere.

Private motor cars are also responsible for another serious environmental problem: **traffic congestion**. Like pollution, traffic congestion is a **negative externality**. Motorists drive cars to achieve private objectives such as travelling from A to B to get to work or to meet friends. But in trying to maximise **private benefit**, congestion (and pollution) are produced, the effects of which are suffered by people other than the individual motorists responsible for these **external costs**. Thus the **social costs** resulting from driving a car, which are borne by the whole community, exceed the private costs incurred by the motorist. In a free-market situation, the incentive function of prices fails to work properly. Because it does not reflect the *true* cost of motoring, which includes the cost of congestion and pollution, the price the motorist pays (the price of petrol, car maintenance, etc.) is too low. It creates the wrong incentive, namely for too much road use, and as a result too many motorists use the roads. To put it another way, excessive road use means that too many of the economy's scarce resources are allocated to private motoring. This is an example of allocative inefficiency and market failure.

Road building and an integrated transport policy

Some people, particularly motorists and the construction industry, believe that to solve congestion problems even more resources should be allocated to motoring. They want many more roads to be built, particularly motorways, bypasses and ring roads around towns. But road building often encourages even more car use, until eventually the new roads are just as congested as the old roads they were built to relieve. Many economists accept the need for *some* extra road building, particularly to improve access to more remote parts of the country, but they generally argue that road building alone is not the solution. Instead they argue for an **integrated transport policy** in which investment in **rail** and **bus** services improves **public transport** to an extent sufficient to attract many private motorists from their cars. But as the experience of recent Labour governments has shown, implementing an integrated transport policy in a densely populated country is not easy. Indeed, in 2000 and 2001, transport *disintegration* rather than *integration* occurred. Chaos on the railways (which was largely the result of the previous Conservative government's ill-thought-out privatisation scheme) has contributed to an even greater use of cars.

Deterring car use

As with road building, simply providing *more* public transport cannot, on its own, reduce traffic congestion. This is most obvious in the case of bus travel. Buses compete with other vehicles for road space. On congested roads, bus journeys are slow and unreliable. In these circumstances, few motorists are willing to abandon their cars and to travel by bus instead. For motorists to switch to public transport on a large scale, private car use must be made much more difficult, particularly in congested areas and at congested times of day.

As with other examples of market failure, **regulation**, **taxation** and **subsidy** are the main policy instruments that UK governments have used to deter car use. Regulations such as **parking restrictions** and **pedestrianised zones** are generally imposed to relieve congestion in town centres. Motorists are taxed in three main ways: at the time of purchase, by the annual vehicle tax and by a tax on fuel. The first of these has almost no deterrent effect on motorists. Because new cars are taxed at exactly the same rate of VAT as other consumer goods, the tax system does not increase their price relative to other goods. And like the **annual vehicle tax**, the **tax on new cars** taxes car *ownership* but not car *use*. By contrast, **fuel taxes** deter car use. The more the car is driven, the greater the total tax paid.

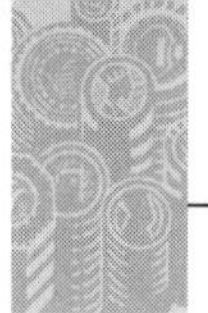

To deter car use, recent UK governments have switched the structure of motoring taxation away from car ownership and the annual vehicle tax towards higher fuel taxes. However, this has aggravated motorists and had little or no effect on car use. The **income elasticity of demand** for private motoring is high, but the **price elasticity of demand** is low. Although fuel taxes are levied at a rate of well over 100%, the low price elasticity of demand means they would have to be very much higher to bring about a significant reduction in demand for car travel. Meanwhile, with continuously rising personal incomes and a high income elasticity of demand, the demand curve for private motoring has shifted significantly rightwards.

In 2000 motorists protested against high fuel prices and fuel taxes by blockading oil refineries. This forced the Labour government to abandon plans for even higher fuel taxation. The success of the fuel price protest means that future UK governments are unlikely to try to raise fuel taxes to a level high enough to have a significant deterrent effect on car use. Alternatively, **relative prices of private and public transport** could be altered by **subsidising public transport**. However, unlike many governments in continental Europe, recent UK governments have generally reduced rather than increased levels of subsidy for public transport.

Road pricing

Apart from their political impracticality, higher fuel taxes have the further disadvantage that they are a blunt instrument, raising the price of car use for *all* motorists, and not just those driving on congested roads. They fall particularly heavily on low-income motorists living in remote rural areas, who tend to be more dependent on their cars than people living in big cities. Rural motorists often have to drive longer distances, yet lack a public transport alternative. Thus, by taxing the rural poor more heavily than the urban rich, higher fuel taxes have adverse **distributional effects** on people's real incomes.

For political and economic reasons, government sentiment has recently swung away from ever higher fuel taxes, towards the idea of **road pricing**. One form of road pricing is already widely used in the UK, namely **charging for parking**. **Tolls** are also charged for using bridges and tunnels. But motorists are not yet charged for driving along ordinary roads. The main *economic* argument against road pricing relates to the **public good properties** that roads sometime possess. First, until the recent development of **electronic road pricing**, roads other than motorways have been generally **non-excludable** because they have a large number of points of entry and exit, which make it impractical to locate barriers or toll gates at every point of access. Second, *uncongested* roads are **non-rival** (or **non-diminishable**) because an extra motorist driving on an almost empty road does not add in any significant sense to road congestion. As with all public goods, there is a case for *not charging a price* for the use of an uncongested road. Provided the road remains uncongested, the **allocatively efficient** amount of road use is the amount motorists choose when granted free access. However, this logic is turned on its head as soon as a road becomes congested. Road use immediately generates negative congestion externalities, which raise the social cost of road use above the private cost incurred by motorists. Without road pricing, motorists pay a price for road use that is now less than the true social cost of their activity. There is therefore a strong economic case for charging motorists for driving on congested roads, while giving them free access to uncongested roads.

If road pricing is introduced, motorists will probably be charged for driving into city centres, and also according to the time of day when their journeys are made. Besides being politically unpopular, road pricing may contribute to the further decline of inner-city shopping areas and to the growth of out-of-town retail parks. Road pricing may also simply shift congestion to new areas where road use is free. (Similarly, if tolls are introduced on British motorways, they may shift traffic back on to roads through towns and villages that the motorways were built to relieve.) On the plus side, road pricing may create a more allocatively efficient division of transport between rail and road. Rail use creates fewer negative externalities than road use. It can be argued that, without road pricing, road use is too cheap compared to rail travel. As a result, too many people travel by road and too few by rail. In theory at least, road pricing can correct this resource misallocation, though some economists argue that rail subsidies are needed as well, to create 'correct' (i.e. allocatively efficient) *relative* prices of road and rail.

The national economy and the environment

Many governments, especially those in richer, developed countries, are explicitly committed to **maintaining and improving the quality of the environment**. However, environmental objectives may not be consistent with achieving the government's main short-term **macroeconomic objectives**, particularly **economic growth**, but also **full employment**, **control of inflation** and a **satisfactory balance of payments**.

Governments wish to maintain and improve the quality of the environment for two main reasons:

(1) The environment contributes significantly to people's standard of living and economic welfare.

(2) The environment affects the sustainability of economic activity. Our ability to produce and consume goods and services in the future will depend in large part upon how we treat the environment now.

The trade-off between environmental objectives and economic growth

If governments could achieve all their policy objectives simultaneously, the 'economic problem' would largely disappear! But conflicts between policy objectives mean it is difficult if not impossible to 'hit' all objectives at the same time. Because they cannot achieve the impossible, policy-makers generally settle for the lesser goal of trading off between policy objectives. A trade-off exists when two or more desirable objectives are mutually exclusive; success in achieving a particular objective or set of objectives is at the expense of a poor and deteriorating performance with regard to other policy objectives. Figure 6 shows the main trade-off facing governments with respect to the conflict between macroeconomic and environmental objectives, namely the trade-off between the two policy objectives of maintaining and improving environmental quality, and maximising the economy's growth rate, measured by GDP growth.

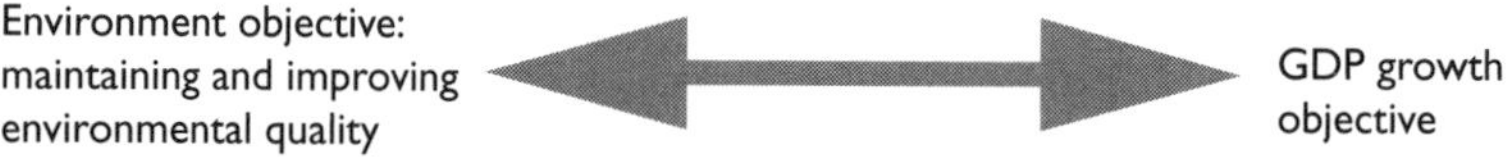

Figure 6 The trade-off between maintaining and improving environmental quality and maximising the economy's growth rate

Economic growth, economic development and the environment

It is important to distinguish between **economic growth** and **economic development**. Economic growth, which can be defined as the **outward movement of the country's production possibility frontier**, is usually measured by the growth of **gross domestic product (GDP)**. Economic development, by contrast, is a wider and deeper process, encompassing two important factors over and above simple GDP growth. First, a significant part of the extra output produced by growth must be used for the benefit of current and future generations of the whole population: for example, through improving health, water supplies and sanitation. Second, development must be **sustainable**, whereas by ignoring the effects on the environment of **resource depletion** and **degradation**, a narrow policy of achieving the fastest possible GDP growth without development is likely to be unsustainable. Properly conceived and pursued, a policy of economic development is 'environment friendly'; the raw pursuit of economic growth *per se* is not.

The conflict between economic growth and economic welfare derived from the environment

The ultimate purpose of economic activity (and hence economic policy) should be to improve economic welfare. With this in mind, it is useful to identify three main components in standards of living and economic welfare:

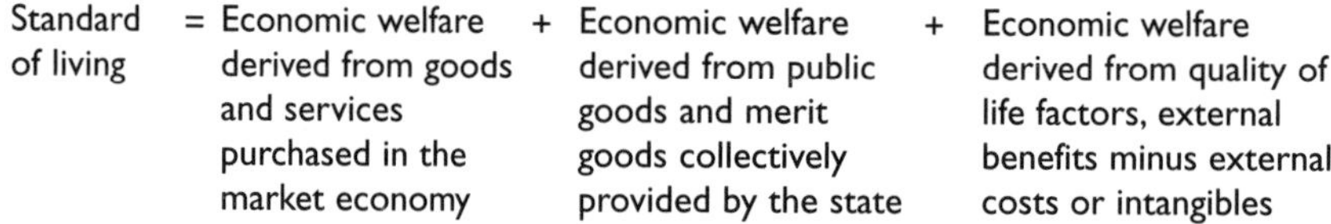

GDP figures are usually used to measure standards of living and economic growth. The problem is that GDP usually captures only the first two of these components of the standard of living, namely the material goods and services produced in the economy. Intangible factors, which are the third element in people's living standards, are ignored. These intangible factors include the value that people place on leisure time and living close to work, and the externalities generated by the production and consumption of national income, which affect people's welfare and quality of life.

If the pursuit of economic growth leads to the destruction of beautiful views and other external benefits conveyed by the environment, while simultaneously creating more pollution and congestion, there has to be a conflict between the government's macroeconomic objectives and its environmental objectives. But in so far as externalities are taken into account in the measurement of GDP growth, what is in effect a welfare loss may be shown as an increase in national output, falsely indicating an apparent welfare gain. For example, the extra time motorists spend in traffic jams caused by increased traffic congestion apparently contributes to economic growth through increased expenditure on petrol and garage services.

The conflict between environmental objectives and full employment

There are a number of ways in which the pursuit of environmental objectives might destroy jobs. First, assuming a slower growth rate, fewer workers would be needed than if the growth rate were higher. Second, the need to comply with environmental regulations and pay pollution taxes would internalise previously external costs of production. Businesses would be forced to pay for costs of production previously dumped as externalities upon third parties. Such compliance costs would probably destroy jobs, particularly if competitors in other countries were not similarly regulated and taxed. And third, jobs would also be lost if, in a process known as **environmental dumping**, multinational companies decided to evade environmental regulations and taxes by relocating polluting or dirty activities in countries with laxer environmental policies. Environmental dumping does, however, create employment in poorer countries — though at the expense of job losses in richer, developed economies.

But it might not all be one-way traffic. Environmental regulation can also create jobs, thereby lessening the conflict between environmental and employment objectives. First, as individuals and nations grow richer, they place a greater value on the quality of the environment in which they live, and demand improvements in environmental quality. Jobs can be created producing goods and services to meet this demand for environmental quality — evidenced by the growth of employment in the organically grown food industry. Second, manufacturing firms in countries with the most demanding environmental regulations, such as Sweden and Germany, have gained a competitive advantage in producing the new technologies to meet the tougher environmental laws and standards. As other countries adopt similar standards, export demand will create jobs in the countries and firms that have led the development of clean technologies.

The conflict between environmental objectives and control of inflation

By raising businesses' costs of production, environmental regulations and taxes might contribute to cost-push inflation. The pursuit of environmental objectives might also raise the inflation rate in other ways. Arguably, by allowing retailers to benefit from economies of scale and other improvements in productive efficiency, the growth of out-of-town shopping centres and superstores has reduced inflationary pressures. However, the UK government has decided to limit any further out-of-town development, having accepted the argument that shopping centres and superstores damage the environment both inside and outside the urban areas they serve.

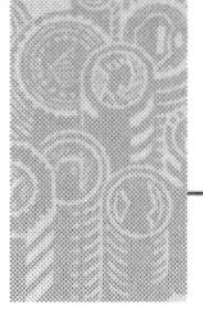

The conflict between environmental objectives and the balance of payments

Many of the factors already mentioned will also affect a country's trading position. The increased business costs that environmental regulations and pollution taxes bring about are likely to reduce international competitiveness, and worsen the balance of payments on current account. Likewise, via the process of environmental dumping, trade can enable polluters to use countries with lax environmental rules as export platforms into markets where standards are higher. Not only does this penalise 'virtuous' companies that decide to remain at home, but also it makes it harder to raise environmental standards. As a result, countries may introduce protectionism to defend themselves against what they see as 'unfair' imports. Free traders believe that this can degenerate into a form of environmental imperialism, in which rich countries ban imports from poor countries, using environmental arguments to cover their own inefficiencies. They argue that free trade helps rather than harms the environment. In part this is because trade makes countries richer, and the rich place a high value on environmental quality and can afford to invest in clean technology.

Examination skills

The skills most likely to be tested by a question on the environment are as follows:

- Explaining how economic activity involves the use of renewable and non-renewable resources, and may lead to both resource *depletion* and resource *degradation*.
- Understanding how firms and consumers can reduce resource depletion (e.g. by recycling) and resource degradation (e.g. by adopting cleaner technologies).
- Identifying and evaluating various ways in which the government can reduce the harmful environmental effects of production and consumption.
- Explaining that government intervention to correct environmental market failures may be unsuccessful, leading sometimes to government failure.
- Identifying and evaluating ways in which household activities such as shopping and the production of waste affect the environment.
- Identifying and evaluating ways in which the government may use taxation, subsidy and regulation to alter economic behaviour.
- Understanding how various forms of transport, particularly road and air transport, use up fossil fuels, create pollution and contribute to problems such as global warming.
- Identifying and evaluating various ways in which the government can attempt to correct market failures relating to the environment (e.g. regulation, taxation, subsidy, road pricing).
- Evaluating the need for and success of the government's integrated transport policy.
- Understanding the government's environmental objectives and how they may conflict with other policy objectives, particularly growth, but also full employment, price stability and trade objectives.
- Understanding the long-term effects on the national economy of failing to protect the environment.

Common examination errors

- Confusion of resource depletion and resource degradation.
- Inability to use appropriate economic terminology, e.g. market failure, allocative efficiency and inefficiency.
- Writing colourful accounts of environmental disasters without any economic analysis.
- Failure to use appropriate diagrams to illustrate the effect of environmental externalities.
- Failure to analyse car and aviation pollution, and road congestion, in terms of negative externalities.
- Failure to apply public good analysis to the case for and against introducing road pricing.
- Use of emotive political arguments (e.g. a motorist's right to drive a car) rather than strictly economic analysis.
- Imprecise analysis of how regulation, taxation, subsidy or road pricing may be used to correct a transport market failure relating to the environment.
- Confusion of short-term and long-term aspects of the relationship between the national economy and the environment.

The economics of sport and leisure

These notes, which relate to AQA specification section 12.3, prepare you to answer AQA examination questions on:

- the demand for sport and leisure
- the supply and pricing of sport and leisure
- competition, monopoly and market failure in sport and leisure markets
- the national economy, the environment and sport and leisure

Demand for sport and leisure

Leisure activities and leisure time

Leisure activities are what people choose to do in **leisure time**. Defined very broadly, leisure time includes all the hours not spent working to earn income or studying. More narrowly and perhaps accurately defined, leisure time should exclude time spent sleeping and performing household and personal chores. Some people — for example, the unemployed and old people — have a large amount of leisure time, but without very much income. As a result, many leisure activities are simply not available to the 'time-rich but money-poor'; the activities are simply too expensive. Indeed, many unemployed people would probably prefer more income (and thus a job) and less leisure time, in order to be able to exercise an **effective demand** (desire backed by an ability to pay) for particular leisure activities. At the other extreme, some people enjoy very little leisure time because

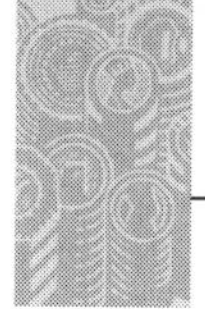

they work very long hours. People who are 'money-rich but time-poor' — for example, those with high-paid City jobs — are often willing to pay large sums of money to enjoy intensively the small amount of leisure time they can squeeze out of a day or weekend.

There are, of course, many leisure activities that are either completely free or virtually free. These include reading a library book, watching television or listening to the radio, and going for a walk.

The demand for leisure time

For most people, leisure time is a **normal good** (a good for which demand increases as income increases). However, most people, unless their income comes from other sources, must work so as to afford the various leisure activities they wish to undertake. High wage rates often encourage people to work longer at the expense of leisure time. But there are exceptions, and for many people there will come a point beyond which they will prefer to enjoy leisure time rather than to work longer hours. Also, many highly paid people enjoy working. Very high hourly wage or salary rates do not necessarily mean that people with high incomes work very short hours in order to enjoy lots of leisure time.

For a person in work, an extra hour of leisure time can mean giving up an hour's pay. The hour's pay is the **opportunity cost** and the **price** of the extra hour of leisure time. The higher the hourly wage rate, the greater the opportunity cost of an extra hour of leisure time.

The demand for particular leisure activities

Different leisure activities are **substitutes** for each other (as are working for pay and enjoying leisure time). A rise in the price of one leisure activity will tend to reduce demand for that activity, as people switch their demand to substitute forms of enjoying leisure time that are now relatively cheaper. When demand for a particular leisure activity such as the cinema is highly **price elastic**, an increase in cinema prices results in a more than proportionate fall in demand. People switch to close substitutes, such as hiring a video or DVD, or watching a film on television, or to completely different leisure activities.

The extent to which different leisure activities are substitutes for each other is measured by **cross elasticity of demand**. A cross elasticity of demand for DVD hire with respect to cinema prices of +0.4 indicates that a 10% increase in cinema prices results in a 4% increase in the demand for DVDs. Although inelastic (i.e. less than 1), this figure would indicate that going to the cinema and hiring a DVD are quite close substitutes. However, consider the case of two football clubs, say Manchester United and Liverpool. For certain floating supporters, the two clubs may be close substitutes, with the supporters switching to whichever team is more successful. But 'true fans' stay completely loyal to one club, regardless of its success or lack of success. For the 'true fan', both price elasticity and cross elasticity of demand with respect to the prices charged by rival clubs can be highly inelastic. Indeed, price and cross inelasticity may extend beyond prices charged to see games, to **complementary goods** such as replica football shirts and other sports **merchandising**.

Shifts of demand for leisure activities

When two leisure activities are substitutes or complementary goods, a change in the price of one leisure activity causes the demand curve for the other to shift. The larger the cross elasticity of demand, the greater is the **shift of demand** for the second leisure activity. Suppose, for example, there is a fall in the price of tickets to see soccer matches (association football). This might lead to a leftward shift of the demand curve for tickets for rugby football matches. This is shown in the left-hand diagram of Figure 7 below. The size of the leftward shift (and of the cross elasticity of demand) will depend on the extent to which, from a spectator's point of view, the two types of football are substitutes for each other. However, a fall in the price of tickets for soccer matches will trigger a rightward shift in the demand curve for complementary goods, such as the replica shirts worn by many spectators. This is shown in the right-hand diagram of Figure 7.

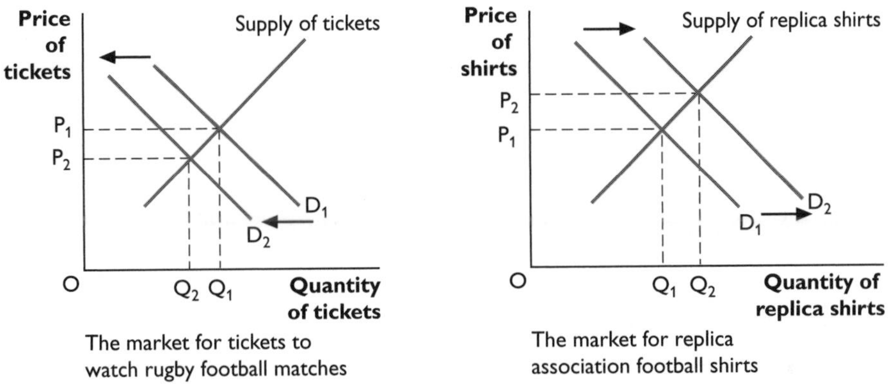

Figure 7 Shifts of demand for substitute and complementary goods, following a fall in admission prices to soccer matches

Income elasticity of demand is another useful concept to apply when explaining and analysing the demand for different leisure activities. We have mentioned that *leisure time* is a normal good for most people. The same is not true for all *leisure activities*. Some are **inferior goods**, for which demand falls as income increases, as people substitute other leisure activities in their place. The activities substituted in their place are normal goods that have a **positive income elasticity of demand**. Some, such as luxury holidays and going to the opera, are also **superior goods** or **luxuries** for which demand increases at a faster rate than income (i.e. income elasticity of demand is greater than +1). By contrast, a leisure activity such as eating out at fast-food restaurants is an inferior good for many people. As income rises, these people prefer smarter and more expensive restaurants to fast-food outlets. For leisure activities that are inferior goods, the income elasticity of demand is negative.

Participation, spectator and elite leisure activities

Leisure activities can be divided into those in which the general public participate in an active sense (**participation activities**) and those that the general public watch (**spectator activities**). Many leisure activities, including sports such as football and

tennis, are available in both forms. For example, people who enjoy the theatre can pay to watch professional actors in the commercial theatre, or they can join a local amateur dramatic society and participate themselves, as either actors or stagehands. Some mass participation leisure activities are available free or virtually free, such as walking or jogging. Likewise, spectating is free or virtually free when restricted to watching television or sport in the local park.

Both participation and spectator leisure activities can be further divided into **elite** and **non-elite** categories. An elite activity may be classified in one of two ways: first, on the basis of cost or the price charged to participate or watch others participating in the activity; and second, on the basis of few people having the talent or aptitude to excel when participating in the activity. A luxury round-the-world cruise is an elite leisure activity on the ground of expense, though no special talent or aptitude is required to buy a ticket for such a cruise. Because of their skills, which few in the population possess, Premiership soccer and international rugby players are elite sportspeople. Also, because of the high ticket prices charged, watching such players ply their trade has increasingly become an elite spectator activity. Certain categories of sailing and yachting are elite in both senses: skill required and expense of participating. At the other extreme, mass participation sports such as angling — which claims to be the UK's most popular participation sport — are very definitely non-elite: virtually anyone can participate at relatively little cost, providing they are prepared to give up the time required.

Supply and pricing

It is useful to distinguish between:

- the initial decision to build **sport and leisure facilities**, such as sports stadiums, fitness centres, cinemas and theatres; and
- the decision to supply a stream of **sport or leisure services** once the facility has been built

With regard to the initial decision to build a sport or leisure facility, some facilities (e.g. a temporary open-air theatre) may be quite easy and cheap to provide, but others (e.g. a super-stadium capable of hosting a World Cup football final or major athletics events) are very expensive to construct. Indeed, as recent aborted attempts to build national football and athletics stadiums in England show, few 'super-facilities' are successfully completed. This is partly because it is very difficult to run sports stadiums and theatres profitably. Construction is usually financed with borrowed funds, on which interest has to be paid. And once complete and operating, large sport and leisure facilities require expensive maintenance and periodic refurbishment. To make a profit, costly facilities need constant use, generating a continuous stream of sales revenue from the box office. But some sports facilities, such as soccer stadiums, are only used once a fortnight, and even then not all the year round. It may be impossible to run such a facility profitably, particularly when the supply of the 'product' that spectators are paying to see, such as a Premiership football team, leads to huge wage costs in addition to the costs of running the stadium.

The more a sport or leisure facility — however big or small — can be used continuously throughout the day, week and year, the more likely it is that the services it provides can be made available commercially at a price that users or spectators can afford and are willing to pay. In the case of major spectator sports, stadium use can be increased by: (1) ground sharing (e.g. Italian soccer clubs such as AC Milan and Inter-Milan); (2) using the stadium for more than one sport (e.g. soccer and rugby) and incorporating hotels, banqueting and conference suites into the stadium (e.g. Chelsea football club); and (3) incorporating other revenue earners into the stadium (e.g. a shop selling club merchandise, or a club museum). But even when better facility usage generates more revenue, it is often impossible to run sports stadiums, theatres and opera houses profitably. The only way leading professional sports clubs can make a profit is by selling rights to televise the sport. Increasingly, the 'supply' of a professional sports match (i.e. the day and time of the event) is determined by television companies and not by clubs or spectators who pay to watch the event live.

The pricing of sport and leisure

One way in which the providers of sport and leisure facilities can increase revenue is by charging different prices, both for different events available at the facility and for different customers. Football clubs charge higher prices for 'big games': for example, against a top club or a local rival. Likewise some theatres charge different prices for different plays or shows. Also, sports fans and theatregoers are charged different prices for seats in different parts of the stadium or theatre. Some seats provide a better view than others, so the quality of the 'product' varies according to where the seat is located. Customers are prepared to pay more for a high-quality view and comfort than for lower quality. Lower prices for children and old age pensioners are a common feature of pricing for sports and leisure events and facility use. A further variant is lower prices for frequent users: for example, in the form of season ticket pricing. London theatres also use a form of 'stand-by' pricing, similar to that used by airlines. Theatregoers can buy tickets at very low prices a few hours before a show, providing there are unsold tickets available. Since the show is being provided anyway, it is better from the theatre's point of view to sell a ticket at a very low price than to have an empty seat in the theatre.

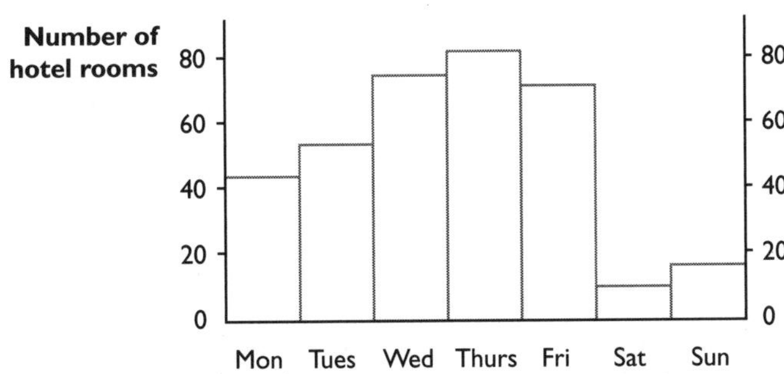

***Figure 8** Hotel room occupancy on different days in the week, assuming the same price is charged throughout the week*

Figure 8 illustrates another way in which sport and leisure industries use pricing to address the problem of unused capacity. The diagram shows the number of rooms occupied in a hotel on different days in the week *assuming that the same price is charged for a room throughout the week*. The diagram shows that, for this hotel, **peak demand** is mid-week (maybe because of business demand), but the weekend is a slack period or **off-peak**. Many hotels try to improve the utilisation of rooms and other hotel facilities in the off-peak period by reducing prices at the weekend to attract families and other tourists. By charging lower off-peak prices, demand can be made more even through the week and capacity can be better utilised. In a similar way, lower prices are charged in the off-peak winter season than in the peak summer season, though for some tourist destinations, such as winter sports resorts, the peak and off-peak seasons are reversed.

Commercial supply, government supply and voluntary sector supply

The **sport and leisure industry** can be defined as the commercial sector of the economy supplying sport and leisure goods and sport and leisure services. Government (both central and local) and the voluntary sector are also involved in the supply of sport and leisure facilities and services. In part this results from the difficulties just described in providing sports commercially at a profit.

To explain the relative importance of commercial, government and voluntary-sector supply of sport and leisure activities, it is useful to distinguish between **collective consumption goods**, **private good substitutes for collective goods** and **pure private goods**. It can be argued that consumers look first to the public sector or government sector for the provision of collective goods such as parks and clean beaches and bathing areas. However, consumers are likely to be dissatisfied with the level and quality of government provision of any particular collective good. As a result they look for additional output in the voluntary sector and the commercial sector. The more uniform the good, the more likely is the government to provide it. The less uniform the good, the more likely is the commercial sector to provide it. The more collective the good, the more likely is any output additional to that provided by the government to be provided by the voluntary sector. The more private and less collective the good, the more likely is the additional output to be provided by the commercial sector.

Any one consumer has little control or influence over key elements of a collectively provided sport or leisure service, such as quality, form, type and time of availability. Desire for individual control increases with income, so the commercial sector tends to 'skim' the market, providing for the needs of higher-income consumers who are prepared to pay a higher price for these key elements. For example, golf attracts high-income consumers, and the commercial sector increasingly provides golf courses and driving ranges. Similarly, the commercial sector provides exclusive health and fitness centres with a greater range of services and facilities than a local authority-run centre can provide. In team sports, the voluntary sector is the most important supplier of amateur sports, while the commercial sector supplies professional sports.

Competition, monopoly and market failure

Competitive markets contain a large number of firms, whereas in its strict meaning, **monopoly** is a market in which there is only one firm. Generally, however, economists use the term *monopoly* rather more loosely, as a market with a *dominant* firm, though not necessarily only one firm. Firms in many markets possess a degree of **monopoly power** (or **market power**). Economists generally agree that if monopolies use their market power to restrict output, raise prices and restrict consumer choice, **market failure** occurs. But they also argue that monopoly can be justified if **economies of scale** lead to lower costs of production and improved **productive efficiency**, or to the **innovation** of new products and more efficient methods of production.

Because there are so many sport and leisure markets, some are highly competitive, but others provide significant evidence of monopoly power. Leisure markets often contain a number of segments or submarkets, some of which are highly competitive, while others contain very few firms. For example, there are thousands of different holiday resorts and travel agents in the travel industry, particularly if we define the industry on an international scale. However, one or two very large companies, such as Thomson Travel Group (a subsidiary of the European company Preussag AG, the world's largest travel company), may dominate significant segments of the industry, such as the mass package holiday industry within the UK, and possess considerable market power. Likewise, there are scores of airlines, but through ownership of landing slots at Heathrow airport, an airline such as BA may possess considerable monopoly power with regard to the lucrative London–New York route.

Some professional sports markets, such as those for football and snooker, provide an interesting mix of competition and monopoly. In football, clubs or teams compete in a league. The purpose of competition is to win the league and to be generally successful from year to year. In most conventional markets, becoming a monopoly by driving rivals out of business represents ultimate success for a firm. But if a soccer club bankrupts all its rivals, there is no one to play against! If Manchester United were to win the Premiership too many times with too much ease, the league would become boring and fans would lose interest. Scottish football, where Celtic and Rangers dominate, has already suffered this problem, though the two leading teams are still well supported. The top teams might seek to solve the problem by abandoning the league, and seeking entry to a new 'super league' where competition promises to be stiffer and the 'market' more interesting for fans.

Football clubs try to purchase success by buying top players from other clubs on the transfer market. But this contributes to the problem just described. Some sports impose special rules or regulations on member clubs to reduce the chance of one club or a handful of clubs dominating the competition. Unlike soccer in the UK, professional American football (the NFL) recruits virtually all its young footballers from American universities and colleges. Under a system known as the draft, NFL clubs that performed poorly in the previous season can recruit the best young players graduating from college football. This increases their chances of being successful.

Many professional sports leagues were originally founded by voluntary associations of clubs, usually decades ago when the sport was amateur or semi-professional. The member clubs decide the rules and regulations of the league — and the extent to which the league is 'competitive' in a business sense. Sports leagues are often highly 'anti-competitive' in the way in which they erect **barriers to entry** that prevent or deter new clubs from joining the league. In the 1970s, the spread of colour television transformed snooker from an unfashionable sport in the UK into a 'big-money' televised sport. At the time, most of the leading professional snooker players were mature players who had dominated major tournaments for several years. Fearing competition from younger players attracted into the game by the prospect of big money, for several years the established players supported restrictive rules that made it difficult for emerging players to enter prestige televised money-spinning competitions such as the World Snooker Championship. These barriers have now been removed and young players currently dominate the game.

Market failure in sport and leisure markets

As well as monopoly and the restriction of competition, sport and leisure markets provide examples of other market failures. These include **public goods**, **externalities** and **demerit** and **merit goods**. Public goods are non-rival and non-excludable. **Non-rival** means that one person's consumption does not prevent another person enjoying the same product at the same time. **Non-excludable** means that if the good is provided for one person, it is provided for all; consumers can't be prevented from enjoying the product. If they so wish, consumers can 'free-ride', i.e. benefit without paying. If too many consumers free-ride, it becomes uneconomic to provide the public good through the market. Hence the market fails and alternative provision is required: for example, through government spending.

Large, natural, land-extensive recreational resources such as mountains, coastlines, lakes and rivers have public good properties, though because people can be excluded, they are not pure public goods. Nevertheless they are largely non-rival (though some would argue that degradation by tourists means this is not so), and it is generally difficult and expensive to exclude free-riders. International sporting success is a more pure form of public good, since it is impossible to exclude people from benefiting from the feeling of national well-being that such success generates. But in many sports, markets alone cannot deliver international success. State provision of facilities and training is often necessary.

Externalities are public *goods* (in the case of **positive externalities** or **external benefits**) or public *'bads'* (in the case of a **negative externality** or **external cost** such as pollution or congestion). Externalities are discharged in the course of production or consumption and received as a **spin-off** effect by **third parties**. The defining feature of an externality is that it is discharged and received outside the market. Externalities provide examples of **missing markets**, since, for example, the owner of a mountain cannot charge for the beautiful view that onlookers many miles away enjoy. Spectator sports provide many similar examples of positive externalities, such as the pleasure enjoyed by people watching a park football match or yachts sailing on a river. Compare also a full theatre or soccer stadium with an almost empty venue. A crowded theatre or stadium creates 'atmosphere'. Part of the pleasure enjoyed by paying spectators stems not from the play or soccer match itself, but from 'crowd reaction'. The spectators provide positive externalities for each other, which increase everybody's enjoyment of the event or spectacle.

Unfortunately, sport and leisure activities also yield negative externalities. Many people drop litter or contribute to traffic congestion when travelling to and from leisure activities and sporting events, and perhaps also contribute to the degradation by human erosion of natural beauty spots. Some anti-social 'leisure' pursuits, such as graffiti 'art' and football hooliganism, provide examples of **demerit goods**. Negative externalities are produced when an individual consumes a demerit good, with the result that the **social costs** suffered by the whole community are greater than the **private costs** incurred by the consumer.

Fortunately, however, sport and leisure activities are usually merit goods rather than demerit goods. Positive externalities are produced when an individual consumes a merit good. As a result, the **social benefits** enjoyed by the whole community exceed the individual consumer's **private benefit**. Additionally, many merit goods possess a second characteristic: the *long-term* private benefits enjoyed by individual consumers are greater than the *short-term* private benefits.

When sport and leisure facilities such as ice rinks are made available to young people, juvenile crime and anti-social behaviour rapidly fall. This is an important example of the first characteristic of a merit good. The second characteristic is illustrated by the fact that participant sports involving physical exercise make people healthier.

When a merit good such as sports playing fields is provided solely through the market, the market fails because too few people consume and enjoy the good's benefits. The reason why is illustrated in Figure 9, where P_1 is the market price charged for the use of commercially provided playing fields. At market prices, playing field use is at the level Q_1, but suppose Q_2 represents the socially optimal level of use. The market fails because the price is too high, deterring consumption. By shifting the supply curve rightward, a subsidy reduces the price that users pay to P_2, thereby correcting the market failure. Consider also a further proposition. Were Q_3 to be deemed the socially optimal level of usage, there would be a case for providing playing fields free of charge to encourage maximum usage. This would justify granting a 100% subsidy to private providers of the playing fields, or the government providing the playing fields and financing collective provision out of general taxation.

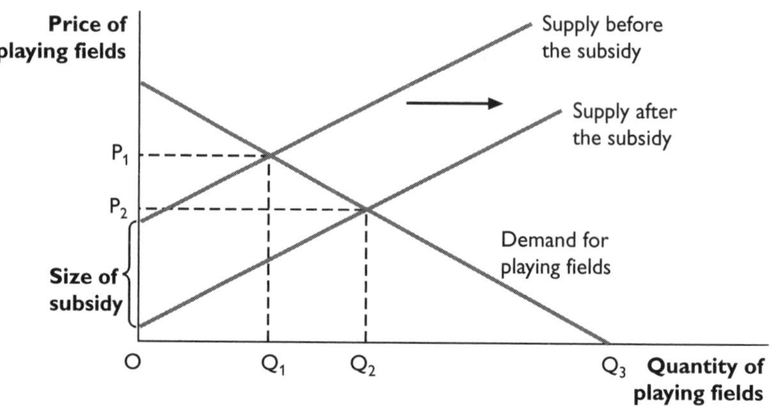

Figure 9 How the granting of a subsidy encourages consumption of a merit good such as sports playing fields

The national economy, the environment and sport and leisure

By improving public health, reducing crime and enhancing a sense of national well-being, government support for sport and leisure activities can have desirable effects on the national economy. For example, labour productivity may increase and absenteeism from work may reduce, thereby freeing resources for alternative and more productive use elsewhere in the economy.

Spending on large sport and leisure facilities, such as the Millennium Dome or a large new football or rugby stadium, is a form of **investment**. It can increase both **aggregate supply** and **aggregate demand**. By adding to the quantity of productive capital in the economy, investment in sport and leisure facilities **contributes to economic growth** and to the **outward movement of the economy's production possibility frontier (PPF)**. This also shifts the economy's **long-run aggregate supply curve (LRAS) from** $\mathbf{LRAS_1}$ to $\mathbf{LRAS_2}$, as illustrated in Figure 10.

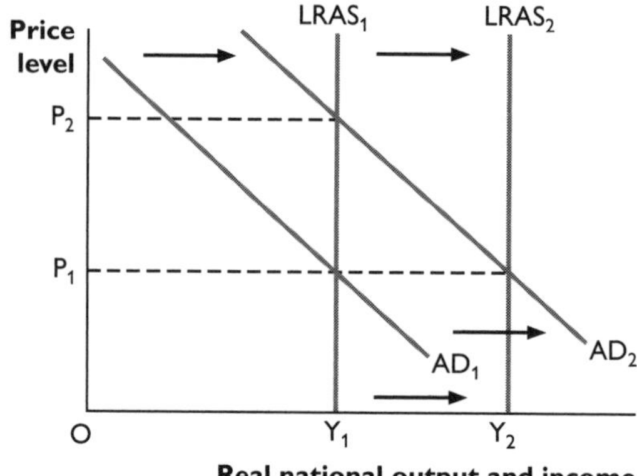

Figure 10 How government spending on sport and leisure may shift AD and AS curves and stimulate national output

But investment spending is also an important component of aggregate demand. As well as increasing aggregate supply, investment in major sport and leisure facilities can shift the aggregate demand curve rightward, from AD_1 to AD_2 in Figure 10. Suppose the economy is initially at full employment (say, at Y_1 in Figure 10). In this situation, whether an increase in spending on sports facilities leads to inflation (and the price level rising above P_1) or mainly increases national output depends on whether the resulting rightward shift of aggregate supply matches the rightward shift of aggregate demand, i.e. whether sufficient extra productive capacity is created to absorb the increase in aggregate demand.

Different analysis is appropriate, however, if initially the economy is producing *inside* its PPF, in which case there are unemployed workers and spare productive capacity. In this situation, investment in a major new sport or leisure complex will trigger a **multiplier** process, whereby total output and income increase by a *multiple* of the initial spending on the sport or leisure complex. The multiplier can be explained in the following way. Suppose £200 million is invested in a major new stadium. This represents income for construction companies, architects and building workers, who in their turn spend *part* but *not all* of the £200 million they receive. Suppose they spend £150 million on **consumption** and **save** the rest. At the next stage in the multiplier process, people working in the production and sale of consumer goods receive the £150 million as income. In their turn, these people will spend *part* but *not all* of the £150 million. The multiplier process continues in this way, so that ultimately the increase in output and income resulting from the initial investment spending can be much larger than the actual amount spent building the sport or leisure facility. The extra spending 'ripples' through the economy, generating extra output, income and spending at each stage in the process. As a result of this stimulation, the economy can expand and recover from a point inside the economy's PPF to a point closer to the frontier.

Spending on major new sport or leisure complexes can also have significant **regional multiplier** effects, stimulating the local economy around the complex. In 2001, Arsenal football club published plans to build a new stadium in north London. If built, not only will the local economy be stimulated, or so Arsenal claims, but there may also be considerable environmental improvement resulting from the regeneration of a **brown-field site** and from extra investment by the club in a new and more environmentally friendly waste disposal station and 'affordable' housing (as well as some luxury housing). Arsenal claims there will be a net economic and environmental gain, though opponents of the scheme argue that jobs will be lost and traffic congestion will increase on match days.

Cardiff's Millennium Stadium (built by the Welsh rugby authorities but used for other sports and pop concerts), Manchester's Commonwealth Games stadium (to be occupied by Manchester City football club after the Games) and the Millennium Dome (built in a depressed part of southeast London) provide examples of similar major investments. Projects such as these could figure in a Unit 3 data-response question. You might argue, for example, that on match days the Millennium Stadium has undoubtedly stimulated trade in the scores of pubs and bars in central Cardiff where

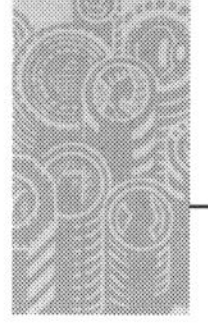

the stadium is situated, but on the cost side, ordinary shoppers avoid central Cardiff on match days, so general retail trade has suffered. Also, some 'mega' projects, most notoriously the Millennium Dome, turn out to be 'white elephants'. As there is insufficient demand for the services that the projects are built to provide, they are commercially unviable, and unable to stay in business without continuous subsidy.

All the projects just mentioned relate to the use of inner-city and brown-field sites. Some major sport and leisure facilities are built instead on **green-field sites**, even sometimes on supposedly protected **green belt** land. On the plus side, out-of-town stadiums may be close to motorways and airports, thus minimising urban congestion on match days, but like out-of-town retail parks and shopping malls, their opponents claim that overall they have an adverse effect on the environment.

A large sports stadium usually takes at least 2 years to build. During this period, costs of construction are incurred but, because the stadium is not being used, sales revenue is not generated. Building is usually financed with borrowed funds, often running to several hundred million pounds. The best time to start construction is during a recession, in the hope that the stadium is ready to use — and generating revenue — just as the economy recovers from recession. During a recession, rates of interest are low and money is therefore cheap to borrow. There is also plenty of spare capacity in the building industry, and construction companies quote much lower prices than they would if the economy were booming. The English Rugby Football Union benefited from building the new Twickenham stadium in the recession of 1990–92, and Arsenal could benefit if the club's new stadium is built when interest rates are at a historically very low level.

Leisure activities unrelated to conventional team sports also have a significant impact on the environment. Arguably the use of mountain bicycles, motor bikes, and four-wheel-drive vehicles 'off road' contributes significantly to soil erosion and general degradation of common land and other rural land. Even relatively benign leisure activities such as going for a walk can have similar adverse effects if too many people visit an area such as the Lake District or Richmond Park in London.

As the international tourist industry grows, similar and perhaps more serious problems are increasing on a global scale. High disposable incomes in the world's richer countries and the increased availability and fall in the real price of air travel are the two main factors promoting the growth of international tourism. Less economically developed countries, of course, want the income that tourists from rich countries bring. Tourism creates jobs for local people, earns vital hard currency and contributes to the development process. But international tourism also creates many problems. It can destroy local cultures and result in a form of 'cultural imperialism' as hamburger joints, night clubs and casinos take over local economies. Many visitors to Ibiza or Nepal may be completely ignorant of and unsympathetic to local traditions. Local beauty spots may be destroyed and crime can proliferate as tourism takes over.

Examination questions may ask for an assessment or evaluation of the benefits and costs resulting from the growth of international tourism. Besides the cultural and environmental effects just noted, there are other important economic effects. Apart from the multiplier effects we described earlier, perhaps the main impact of international tourism is on the **balance of payments**. International tourism contributes to **international trade**. It is a part of **trade in services** (sometimes called **invisible trade**) which, along with trade in goods (or visible trade), makes up the **current account** of the balance of payments. In recent years, tourism has become one of the main **service industries** in a large number of countries, rich and poor, including the UK. The UK has a balance of trade deficit in tourism, resulting from the fact that British residents spend more on holidays abroad than visitors from overseas spend in the UK.

As well as receiving substantial benefits from international tourism (such as the boost to London's theatre land), richer countries such as the UK also suffer adverse economic and other consequences. These include increased noise and atmospheric pollution resulting from the expansion of airports such as Heathrow, and the introduction of pests and diseases into the country. However, richer countries don't suffer to any extent the cultural imperialism that destroys local traditions in poorer countries. But all countries, rich and poor, can suffer from over-dependence on tourism, particularly if an unexpected event or 'outside shock' hits the economy and overseas visitors stop arriving. In the UK, the foot and mouth epidemic and the spin-off of the 'Twin Towers' terrorist attack in New York both caused sudden and unexpected falls in the number of incoming tourists in 2001.

Examination skills

The skills most likely to be tested by a question on the economics of sport and leisure are as follows:

- Explaining the factors determining the demand for, and the supply of, leisure time and/or for particular leisure activities.
- Applying key terms related to demand and supply theory: adjustments along curves, shifts of curves, elasticity etc.
- Discussing the extent to which different leisure activities are substitutes or complements for each other.
- Analysing and explaining the determination of price in sport and leisure markets.
- Showing understanding of the reasons for different forms of supply: commercial, government and voluntary sector supply.
- Assessing the extent to which particular sport and leisure markets are competitive or tending towards monopoly.
- Identifying and explaining particular features of competition in different sport and leisure markets.
- Understanding that governments both provide and subsidise sport and leisure facilities and activities to correct market failures.
- Explaining how expenditure on sport and leisure is a part of aggregate demand, and can also improve supply-side performance and shift the long-run aggregate supply curve rightward.
- Analysing and evaluating multiplier effects resulting from major investment projects in the sport and leisure industry such as the Millennium stadium in Cardiff.

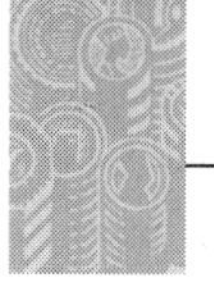

- Understanding how both improvements in the quality of the environment and environmental degradation can affect leisure markets, particularly tourism markets.

Common examination errors

- Confusing the demand for leisure time with the demand for particular leisure activities.
- Inability to use appropriate supply and demand diagrams to analyse sport and leisure markets.
- Failure to distinguish appropriately between participation and spectator leisure activities.
- Failure to understand the reasons for voluntary and government sector provision of sport and leisure facilities and services.
- Failure to explain how sports and leisure businesses can sometimes use their market power in undesirable ways.
- Wrongly asserting that all sport and leisure facilities and activities provided by government are public goods.
- Inability to understand that some leisure activities are better regarded as demerit goods rather than merit goods.
- Failure to understand that expenditure on sport and leisure can increase both aggregate demand and aggregate supply.
- Inability to distinguish between the consumption and investment components of spending on sport and leisure.
- Failure to recognise balance of payments effects and regional multiplier effects of spending on sport and leisure.

Questions & Answers

This section includes nine examination-style questions designed to be a key learning, revision and exam preparation resource. All the questions are data-response questions (DRQs). There are three questions on each of the three options.

The main themes covered by the questions are indicated by the question titles. These are:

The section also includes:

- a student's answer of grade A to C standard for each question
- examiner's comments on each student's answer, explaining — where relevant — how the answer could be improved and a higher grade or mark achieved. These comments are denoted by the icon *e*.

Note: The marks at the end of the examiner's comments for each question and part of each question are the marks awarded by the examiner at the time of marking the question. The total mark for each question in the Unit 3 examination is 40. At a later stage in the examining process, these 'raw marks' are converted into uniform standardised marks, for which each question in the Unit 3 examination has a total of 90 marks. The marks published by the examining board when candidates receive their results are the uniform standardised marks (USM). Uniform standardised marks have the same grade boundaries for all subjects and all unit exams. These are: grade A: 80%; grade B: 70%; grade C: 60%; grade D: 50%; grade E: 40%. These grade boundaries only apply after the raw marks awarded by the examiner have been converted into uniform standardised marks. Because the marks at the end of each question in this guide are raw marks and not standardised marks, the USM grade boundaries listed above have *not been used* to decide the grade that the candidate's answer merits.

Housing, taxation and savings

Total for this question: 40 marks

Study **Extracts A**, **B** and **C**, and then answer **all** parts of the question which follows.

Extract A Owner-occupancy in the UK housing market

The UK now has one of the highest rates of owner occupancy of its housing stock in the world. The favourable tax treatment given to house ownership by successive British governments is one of the factors favouring owner occupancy. Unlike wealth assets such as stocks and shares, the capital gain on housing is largely exempt from tax. When property prices are rising, the owner-occupier who sells a house pockets all the gain in value, tax-free.

UK house-buyers usually borrow a large fraction of the money needed by mortgaging their properties. Until quite recently, owner-occupiers benefited from considerable tax relief on the interest paid on their mortgage loans. When combined with the exemption of most housing from capital gains tax, this meant that house purchase proved to be one of the most rewarding and safe forms of personal investment available to UK households. As a result, for many decades savings were diverted away from alternative investment channels such as the share market and British industry, and into owner occupancy.

The fact that people borrow large sums to finance house purchase gives owner-occupiers a vested interest in the continuation of 'house-price inflation'. When house prices are rising, the value of the house goes up, but the mortgage does not. In fact, the real value of mortgage debt falls, being eroded by the rate of general inflation, measured by the RPI. As a result, with rising house values and declining financial liabilities, owner-occupiers grow wealthier. Householders' growing wealth then leads to a process known as 'equity withdrawal' or 'equity leakage'. By taking out larger mortgages secured against the increased value of their properties, house owners convert wealth, previously held in the form of illiquid bricks and mortar, into money which can be spent on consumption. This process contributes to the continuation of rising house prices and boom conditions in the UK economy.

Source: adapted from *Economics for Professional and Business Studies* (DPP, 1993).

Extract B Paltry savings

The last time the household savings ratio was as low as 3% was in 1988 during the 'Lawson boom'. Increased taxes on saving have been blamed for the low savings ratio. However, the recent fall in the UK savings ratio has much more to do with increased spending on consumption, financed by borrowing. Over the last few years, people have been withdrawing equity in housing to finance extra spending — with good reason. Net household worth is 40 per cent higher now than 4 years ago. House-price inflation exceeding the rate of general inflation has made owner-occupiers richer.

Source: adapted from the *Financial Times*, 28 September 2000.

Extract C The household savings ratio

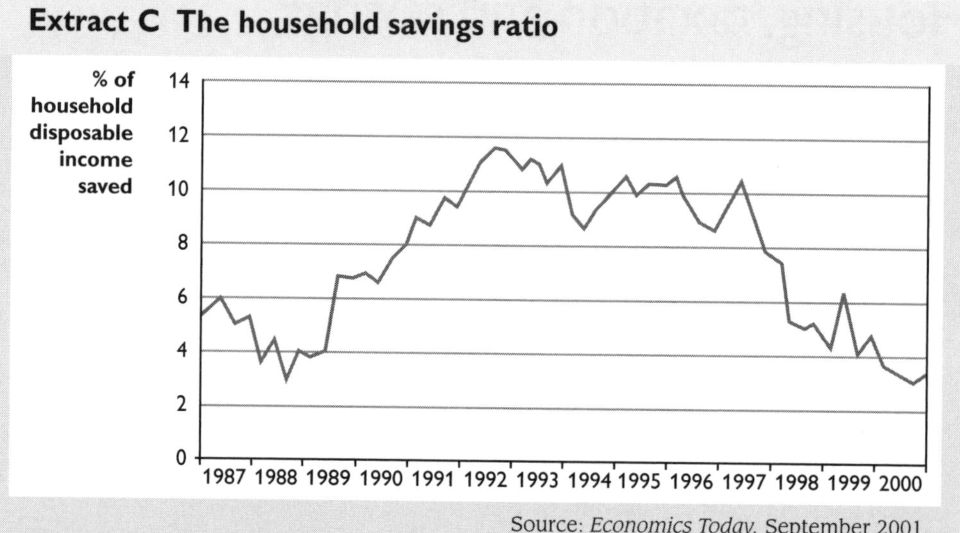

Source: *Economics Today*, September 2001.

(a) What is meant by the term 'capital gain' (Extract A, line 4)? (3 marks)

(b) Describe the main changes in the household savings ratio shown in Extract C. (4 marks)

(c) Explain how house-price inflation may have caused the changes in the household savings ratio described in Extract B and illustrated in Extract C. (8 marks)

(d) With the help of a supply and demand diagram, explain TWO significant causes of house-price inflation in the UK in the late 1980s or late 1990s. (10 marks)

(e) Identify and evaluate the effects on the UK economy resulting from the diversion of household savings away from alternative investment channels, such as the share market and British industry, into the housing market. (15 marks)

■ ■ ■

Candidate's answer

(a) A capital gain is the difference between the price paid for a wealth asset such as a house and the price received when the house is sold at a later date at a higher price.

> *e* This is an example of an answer written by a candidate who obviously knows the meaning of the concept she has been asked to define. For a capital *gain* to occur, a wealth asset must go up in value between the date at which the asset was bought and the date at which it is sold. To *realise* a capital gain, the asset must be sold. By contrast, a house owner who decides not to sell a property that has gone up in value, benefits from an *unrealised* capital gain. **3/3 marks**

(b) The household savings ratio, which shows savings as a percentage of total disposable income, varied between a low of about 3% towards the beginning and end of the data, and a high of nearly 12% in 1992 and 1993. The changes in the household savings ratio are related to the phases of the business cycle: people save more in recessions than in boom periods.

This answer earns 3 of the available 4 marks — she needed to make a clear statement that over the whole period, the savings ratio fell, then rose, then fell again, to earn full marks. The question asks for a description. With a question like this, don't drift into an explanation of the causes of the changes you describe. In this case the candidate just about avoided this temptation. **3/4 marks**

(c) People save for a number of reasons. These include, first, the desire to accumulate wealth and, second, the precautionary motive to guard against an uncertain and risky future. Because the rate of house-price inflation has usually been higher than the rate of general inflation, owner-occupiers have become wealthier. This has reduced their need to save out of current income, again for two reasons. First, rising household wealth brought about by house-price inflation has reduced the need to save to add to wealth. Second, because rising house prices have promoted a 'feel-good factor', owner-occupiers have viewed the future more confidently. The need to save for precautionary reasons has been reduced. These explanations are reinforced by a third factor. Rising house prices mean that house buyers must take out ever larger mortgages to enable them to purchase ever more expensive properties. Borrowing represents negative saving or dissaving. Other things being equal, an increase in mortgage debt must reduce the ratio of savings to income.

For a question like this at AS, one explanation developed in some depth, or two explanations developed rather more superficially, will usually earn full marks. In this case, the candidate has confidently provided three convincing explanations, so full marks should have been assured. However, she earns 7 marks and not the maximum of 8 marks because nowhere in her answer does she make any reference to what Extracts B and C respectively describe and show, namely a significant fall in the household savings ratio over most of the period shown in the data. **7/8 marks**

(d) House-price inflation in the UK has been caused primarily by demand factors rather than by supply factors. This is illustrated in the following diagram, in terms of the demand curve for housing shifting rightward up an inelastic supply curve of housing, causing the price of housing to rise from P_1 to P_2.

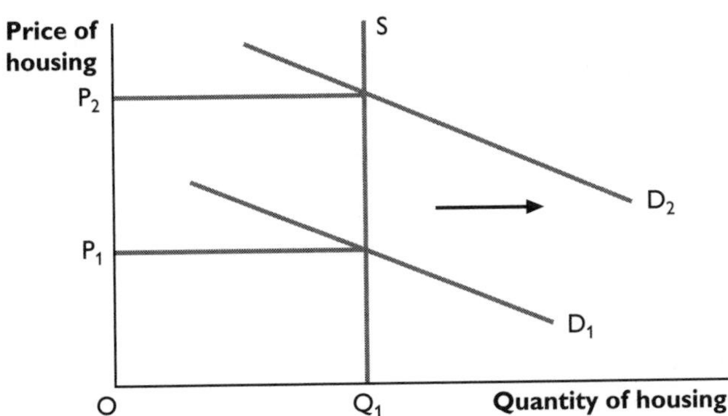

One of the factors causing the demand curve to shift rightward is the speculative nature of the demand for housing. People buy houses as an investment. When house

prices start to rise, people believe they can make capital gains by buying property. This fuels a 'bandwagon' effect in which more people rush to buy property, because they are scared they will miss out if they don't. This causes a further rise in house prices, which in turn induces another rightward shift of demand, and so on.

The candidate has written an excellent explanation of ONE cause of house-price inflation. However, as the question clearly asks for TWO causes, she can only earn half the available marks. You must read the question and obey the key instruction!

5/10 marks

(e) The long-term economic success of the British economy depends on competitiveness and investment by industry in more and better capital equipment. Most goods and services are produced by private-sector companies. British companies can only be competitive in UK and export markets if they have a high rate of investment in machinery etc. This requires finance. Firms need to acquire household savings (by borrowing or share issues) to finance the purchase of capital goods, i.e. investment.

Over many decades, Britain has had a lower rate of investment than similar countries. Many economists argue that this has been a major cause of Britain's lack of competitiveness and relatively poor economic performance, though in recent years there has been some 'catch-up'. Arguably, an important factor explaining low investment by industry has been the tendency for households to direct their savings into housing rather than into financing businesses. The favourable tax treatment given to spending on housing compared to buying shares in companies is largely to blame.

But is this completely true? Economists must look at demand as well as supply. For investment to take place, businesses must *wish to borrow* household savings and/or to make new issues of shares to raise finance that way. It can be argued that low UK rates of industrial investment have had much more to do with the unwillingness of businesses to raise money from households than with the fact that the supply of household saving has been directed into the housing market rather than into the stock exchange and new issues of shares. Also, for most of the 1990s until 2000, share prices boomed. During this period, households were very willing to buy shares and to lend to industry, though at the same time the housing market also boomed.

This is an excellent answer, most definitely of Level 5 (analysis and evaluation) quality. The answer nearly merits full marks but not quite. The candidate is extremely strong on *evaluation*, but she does not display quite enough of the other skill needed for full marks, namely *analysis*. She has *identified* possible effects on business investment, competitiveness and economic performance, though she might have expanded a little on these with some analysis. The real strength of her answer lies in evaluation. Although partly agreeing with the question, the candidate also takes issue with its central assertion. **14/15 marks**

Scored 32/40 80% = grade A

The house-price cycle

Total for this question: 40 marks

Study **Extracts A**, **B** and **C**, and then answer **all** parts of the question which follows.

Extract A Boom and bust in the UK housing market

Many factors conspired to produce the house-price boom of the late 1980s. At the beginning of the boom, household debt levels were low, i.e. mortgage and credit-card debt was low as a ratio of household wealth. Real house prices were also low. There was thus scope for increases in both debt levels and real house prices. Disposable income growth after the early 1980s recession was strong, as were income growth expectations. Wealth to income ratios grew and the spendability of illiquid assets was enhanced by financial liberalisation. Financial liberalisation also permitted higher gearing levels, i.e. borrowing and debt to increase as a ratio of wealth assets. Demographic trends were favourable with stronger population growth in the key house-buying age group. The supply of houses was more inelastic with the stock of housing growing more slowly than demand. Construction of social housing fell to a small fraction of its level in the 1970s. Finally, in 1987–88 interest rates fell and the proposed abolition of property taxes (i.e. rates) in favour of a poll tax gave a further impetus to house-price growth.

However, the bust that followed in the early 1990s was the result of the reversal of most of these factors. With a 'feel-bad' factor replacing a 'feel-good' factor, not even the major falls in nominal interest rates that took place in the early 1990s, while real interest rates remained high, were sufficient to revive UK house prices.

Source: adapted from an academic paper by John Muellbauer and Anthony Murphy, 'Booms and busts in the UK housing market', 31 March 2000.

Extract B Changes in real house prices, 1970–2000

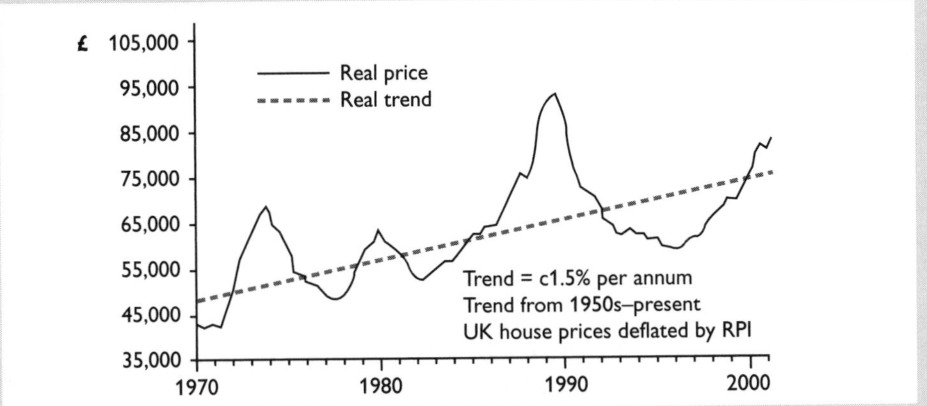

Source: *Nationwide Building Society Website, 31 August 2001.*

question

Extract C Is the house-price cycle being repeated?

Some commentators feared that history would repeat itself when confidence returned to the housing market in the late 1990s, namely a new unsustainable boom in house prices followed by a crash. However, various factors reduce the likelihood of a damaging 'boom and bust' similar to that in the previous cycle. Three dampening forces are operating on the current upturn: less favourable demographic trends, relatively high levels of debt and relatively high real interest rates. To this, one can add the greater awareness by mortgage lenders of default risk and, by the authorities, of the UK housing market as a potential factor in macroeconomic instability.

On the other hand, there are signs of the former being forgotten in some quarters and the Monetary Policy Committee is currently constrained by the strength of sterling and the outcry over plant closures in manufacturing. Nevertheless, 'boom and bust' might occur. Effective financial wealth relative to income is currently close to the high point of the last 35 years and the effects of this are not yet fully reflected in the market. Furthermore, the closest thing the UK has to a property tax — council tax — is poorly related to market values, and therefore dampens house prices less than previous property taxes.

If a house-price boom does occur, it will almost certainly trigger a consumer-spending boom. However, it is a two-way process: changes in house prices affect the economy, but the economy also affects house prices.

Source: adapted from an academic paper by John Muellbauer and Anthony Murphy, 'Booms and busts in the UK housing market', 31 March 2000.

(a) What is meant by 'mortgage debt' (Extract A, line 2)? (3 marks)

(b) What does Extract B indicate happened to real house prices in the UK between 1988 and 2000? (4 marks)

(c) Explain how financial liberalisation (Extract A, line 7) may affect house prices. (8 marks)

(d) With the help of a diagram, explain the statement: 'the supply of houses was more inelastic with the stock of housing growing more slowly than demand' (Extract A, lines 10–11). (10 marks)

(e) Evaluate the ways in which changes in house prices affect the economy and in which changes in the economy affect house prices. (15 marks)

■ ■ ■

Candidate's answer

(a) Most people who buy houses have to borrow a large part of the money they need from a bank or building society. Unlike many other loans, for example credit-card loans, house-purchase loans are secured on the value of the house. The house acts as collateral for the loan. Sometimes banks and building societies repossess houses and kick their occupiers into the street, when they fall behind on interest payments. When loans are secured in this way, the house is said to be mortgaged.

While the candidate obviously knows quite a lot about mortgages, his answer only partially answers the question. Nowhere does he state that mortgage debt is the *stock* of outstanding debt owed by property owners to all the financial institutions that grant loans secured against the property. The answer needs more focus.

2/3 marks

(b) An increase in real house prices means that, on average, house prices rise faster than the rate of general inflation. As Extract B shows, in real terms house prices were at their highest in 1988 at the height of the 'Lawson boom'. In the recession of the early 1990s house prices then fell in real terms, bottoming out in 1996, before rising again in the boom of the late 1990s.

This is an excellent answer, displaying good use of the data and a sound understanding of the meaning of real house prices. The candidate has written enough for full marks, though some reference to the trend rate of growth of real house prices (1.5% a year) would have added to the answer. **4/4 marks**

(c) As I stated in my first answer, most house buyers have to borrow money on a mortgage to finance the purchase of a property. If the *supply* of mortgage finance increases, this causes the *demand* curve for housing to shift rightward. Many years ago, building societies — the financial institutions that provide the largest part of mortgage finance — were heavily regulated. Over-regulation prevented them from competing for new business. Then they were partially deregulated. This liberalised the market for mortgage finance, which in turn triggered a lot of competition amongst building societies and banks for new mortgage business. As a result, the demand curve for housing shifted rightward, and a boom in house prices occurred.

The candidate has explained fully one way in which financial liberalisation has affected house prices. An alternative route to full marks would be to explain how increased competition amongst banks and building societies affects the *price* of mortgage finance as well as its *availability*. The rate of interest is of course the price of mortgage finance. Falling interest rates increase the demand for mortgages and thence the demand for owner occupation. **8/8 marks**

(d) The price elasticity of supply of housing measures the extent to which the supply of housing changes, following a change in the price of housing. It is measured by the following formula:

$$\text{price elasticity of supply of housing} = \frac{\text{\% change in quantity of housing supplied}}{\text{\% change in price of housing}}$$

If, for example, a 10% increase in price induced only a 5% increase in supply, the elasticity of supply would be 0.5, or inelastic. The supply curve drawn in the diagram below is inelastic. When the demand curve shifts rightward from D_1 to D_2, the supply of housing increases less than proportionately.

The extent to which the supply of housing is inelastic depends in part upon the time period under consideration. Supply is more inelastic in the short run than in the long run, and completely inelastic in the very short run when the supply of housing cannot be changed at all.

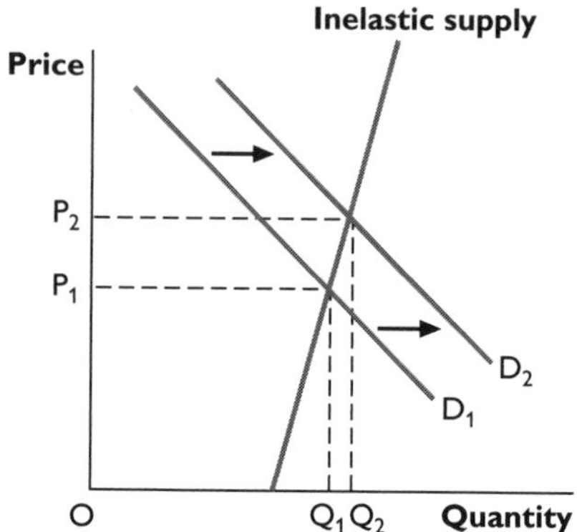

Inelastic supply of housing in the housing market

It is always a good idea to explain a key concept or a technical term in a question. The candidate obviously understands elasticity and includes a correct definition and the formula for measurement in his answer. Likewise, his answer is relevant and accurate. (When a question explicitly asks for a diagram, you must draw one. The mark scheme states that answers must be restricted to a maximum of half the available marks if there is no relevant diagram.) Nevertheless, the candidate does not quite earn full marks because he makes no reference to the *stock* of housing. The stock of housing includes every residential property in the country. It can increase if new houses are built, if houses are divided up into smaller housing units, or if non-residential properties are converted to housing. The housing stock can decrease if houses are demolished or converted to other forms of use. It takes time to change the stock of housing in response to price changes and hence supply tends to be inelastic. **8/10 marks**

(e) There are a number of ways in which changes in house prices affect the economy. One way is through a 'wealth effect'. When house prices are rising faster than the general rate of inflation, house owners become wealthier. Wealth is an important determinant of consumption. Rising house prices therefore lead to an increase in consumer spending, which increases aggregate demand. What happens next depends on the aggregate supply curve. If it is upward sloping, output and employment both rise, though there will also be some inflation. But when full capacity is reached, the AS curve is vertical, so excess demand pulls up the price level in a demand-pull inflation. An adverse effect of rising house prices relates to labour mobility. Housing in London and the southeast may become unaffordable for people in other parts of the UK, deterring the movement of labour to the more prosperous parts of the country.

My earlier answers have already indicated some of the ways in which changes in the economy may affect the housing market, i.e. through the impact of monetary policy and through changes in consumer confidence. I have also mentioned that the onset of recession is likely to affect housing markets adversely. Unemployment and the fear of unemployment and falling or stagnant incomes reduce the demand for housing. People may trade down to smaller properties, or cancel or postpone moving to bigger houses. Likewise, construction companies will sit on their land banks and cancel or postpone starting new housing developments and estates.

The candidate identifies and briefly explains effects or consequences relating to both issues posed by the question. But to earn a high mark, the answer needs to show evidence of 'higher-order' skills: analysis and evaluation. While there is some analysis in the answer (analysis being the critical skill required to reach Level 4), the skill of evaluation is not really displayed. Therefore the answer does not reach Level 5 (13 to 15 marks). Overall the answer reaches low Level 4.

Perhaps the candidate ran out of time. In part he dealt with the shortage of time by making reference to relevant points made in earlier answers. Some examiners might give credit for this, but it is best to try to make answers self-contained, i.e. to avoid cross-referencing to answers to other parts of the question.

10/15 marks

Scored 32/40 80% = grade A

Microeconomic and macroeconomic aspects of UK housing markets

Total for this question: 40 marks

Study **Extracts A**, **B** and **C**, and then answer **all** parts of the question which follows.

Extract A An imperfect housing market

According to Geoffrey Meen, an economist specialising in housing, housing markets have been subject to more market imperfections than almost any other good. Meen identifies the following factors as contributing, or as having contributed, to market imperfections in housing markets:

- the absence of substitute goods for owner-occupied housing
- rent controls
- the fact that housing markets are highly localised (indeed, each house must stand on a separate plot and hence by definition of location no two houses can be the same)
- tax relief previously paid to owner-occupiers
- high transaction costs involved in buying and selling houses

Extract B Stock of dwellings in the UK by tenure

Tenure	End of 1979		End of 1989		End of 1999	
	Thousands	%	Thousands	%	Thousands	%
Owner occupied	11,605	54.7	15,168	65.2	17,157	68.2
Rented from local authorities	6,713	31.6	5,356	23.1	4,107	16.3
Rented privately	2,915	13.7	2,089	8.9	2,708	10.8
Rented from housing associations etc.	—	—	661	2.8	1,171	4.7
Total dwellings	**21,233**	**100**	**23,274**	**100**	**25,143**	**100**

Extract C The macroeconomic impact of housing markets

Economists study housing markets not only because of their inherent importance to individuals, but also because of their general impact on the broader economy. Housing represents one of the largest sectors of spending within the economy. Approximately one of every seven pounds spent in the UK each year is directly related to housing. The significance of this direct housing expenditure is amplified further by the relationship between rising property values and general consumer spending.

'Wealth effects', consumer confidence, 'feel-good factors' and opportunities for equity withdrawal all contribute to the fact that rising house prices are associated with increased consumer spending, particularly on goods which are in joint demand or complementary goods.

According to Professor Andrew Oswald of Warwick University, changes in unemployment have much to do with the housing market. He argues that increased levels of owner occupation have caused people to stay put, whilst an ever-changing world requires workers to move around to search for new jobs. Private rental housing therefore helps, since it allows people to be mobile. According to Professor Oswald's hypothesis, the rise in unemployment between the 1950s and 1990s could be linked to the rise in owner occupancy and the decline in rental tenure, and likewise the more recent fall in unemployment to 6% might be linked to the growth in rental opportunities.

Source: all items adapted from an article by Danny Myers in *Developments in Economics*, Vol. 17 (Causeway Press, 2001).

(a) With the use of an example, explain what is meant by the term 'market imperfections' (Extract A, line 2). (3 marks)

(b) Describe the main changes in housing tenure in the UK between 1979 and 1999 that are shown in Extract B. (4 marks)

(c) Explain how tax relief previously paid to owner-occupiers and high transactions costs involved in house sales may affect the efficiency of housing markets. (8 marks)

(d) Lines 8–10 of Extract C state that 'rising house prices are associated with increased consumer spending, particularly on goods which are in joint demand or complementary goods'. With the help of a diagram, explain this relationship between the price of housing and the demand for complementary goods. (10 marks)

(e) Evaluate the view stated in Extract C that changes in unemployment in the UK have been caused by changes in the availability of rented housing. (15 marks)

■ ■ ■

Candidate's answer

(a) Market imperfections are features of a market that reduce the competitiveness of the market. In many markets, consumers possess imperfect knowledge of the characteristics of goods and of the prices being charged by all the firms or suppliers in the market.

e This answer is short but to the point, showing that the candidate understands the key concept being tested by the question. As she provides a clear and accurate example, she earns full marks. Other examples she might have provided include the exercise of monopoly or market power, producer sovereignty (or lack of consumer sovereignty), and barriers preventing customers or suppliers entering or leaving markets. **3/3 marks**

(b) Over the period shown by the data, owner occupation increased in relative importance while renting from local authorities and private renting both decreased in relative importance. Renting from housing associations, a type of tenure which possibly did not exist in 1979, increased over the twenty-year period, but was by a long way the least significant type of housing.

While identifying the most important *proportionate* changes shown by the data, the answer needs to go further to earn more than 2 marks. The candidate should include at least three or four statistics selected from Extract B to illustrate the growth in importance of owner occupation and the decline of renting as a form of tenure. Reference should also be made to the absolute changes in housing tenure as well as to the proportionate or percentage changes. **2/4 marks**

(c) The tax subsidy paid to previous owners refers to the income tax relief an owner-occupier used to be able to claim, if the house was mortgaged and the owner was paying interest on the mortgage loan. This tax subsidy made housing a more attractive investment than alternatives such as stocks and shares. As a result the demand for housing was higher than it would have been in the absence of the subsidy, as were house prices.

Transaction costs are the costs incurred when making a transaction, i.e. buying something. 'Shoe leather costs' are one type of transaction cost. These are costs of the time spent (and literally the shoe leather worn out) when going from estate agent to estate agent to compare availability and prices of houses. The other transaction costs are legal fees, a tax known as stamp duty levied on each house purchase and the cost of a survey, some of which are incurred even if the sale falls through. In total these can amount to more than £5,000 when purchasing a house.

While this answer shows lots of relevant knowledge and understanding of tax relief and transactions costs, it ultimately disappoints. This is because the candidate fails to apply her knowledge and understanding to address the key issue posed by the question: how the tax relief and transaction costs affect the *efficiency* of housing markets. Full marks could be gained by explaining how both of these distort the housing market adversely. Some transaction costs unnecessarily raise the cost of buying or selling a house. This is *productively inefficient*. And if tax relief increases the demand for housing relative to the demand for other goods, a misallocation of resources results. This is *allocatively inefficient*. **4/8 marks**

(d) The relationship between an increase in the price of housing and the demand for complementary goods such as furniture is measured by cross elasticity of demand. The cross elasticity of demand between complementary goods is normally negative, meaning that a *rise* in the price of housing should lead to a *fall* in the demand for goods that go with housing because fewer houses are demanded. The fact that this does not happen in the markets for housing and goods which are in joint demand with housing can be explained with reference to the diagrams below:

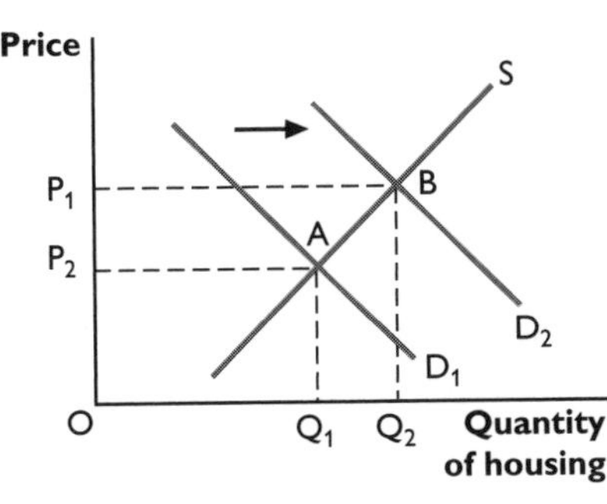

The housing market

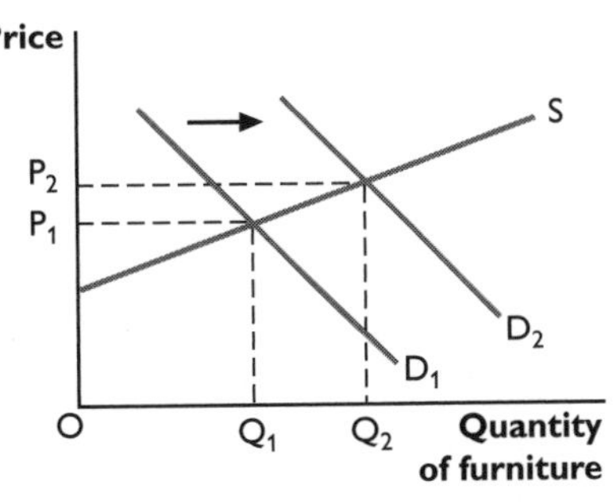

The market for furniture

The left-hand diagram shows the price of housing rising because the demand curve for housing has shifted rightward. More houses are bought at the new equilibrium at point B than at the old equilibrium at point A. This causes the demand curve for complementary goods such as new kitchens, bathrooms and furniture also to shift rightward, as shown in the right-hand diagram.

This is a brilliant answer, showing full understanding of shifts of demand and supply curves, of adjustments to new equilibrium situations, and of how changes in one market can affect another market. The candidate makes use of her knowledge of the rather difficult concept of cross elasticity of demand and her reference to cross elasticity is wholly relevant. Nevertheless, it would be possible to gain full marks without applying explicitly the concept of cross elasticity of demand. **10/10 marks**

(e) Professor Oswald's view, quoted in Extract C, is that when owner occupancy replaces rented accommodation, unemployment rises. Conversely, when more rented accommodation becomes available, unemployment falls. My view (which is probably the same as Professor Oswald's) is that changes in the nature of housing tenure can explain *some* of the changes in unemployment that have occurred, but obviously not *all* the changes.

Ease of obtaining suitable housing affects the geographical mobility of labour. Availability of affordable rented accommodation increases the geographical mobility of labour; by contrast the growth of owner occupancy reduces the mobility of labour. This is partly due to the transaction costs of moving house when moving to a new job (I explained transaction costs in my previous answer). But this is not the whole story. House prices are much higher in London and the southeast of the UK than they are in regions of high unemployment. This difference in regional house prices means that when jobs become available in London, many unemployed workers in, say, Scotland cannot even contemplate moving to London to fill the vacancies because they cannot afford to buy houses in the southeast. By contrast, if plenty of rented housing became available in all regions, the resulting improvement in labour mobility would reduce unemployment significantly.

The flexibility of the housing and labour markets affects the performance of the supply side of the economy. Increased availability of affordable rented

accommodation can be a factor facilitating the rightward movement of the economy's long-run aggregate supply (LRAS) curve. Likewise, flexible housing and labour markets promote faster economic growth and the outward movement of the economy's production possibility frontier. The performance of the supply side of the economy improves and unemployment falls.

However, this analysis depends on the assumption that unemployment is caused by friction and structural rigidity in the economy's aggregate labour market. But often unemployment has other causes, in particular changes in the aggregate demand associated with the business cycle. In 2001, many economists believed that after 9 years of continuous growth, the UK economy was about to enter recession. The growth of unemployment caused by the collapse of demand in a recession has little to do with the state of the housing market. Nevertheless, increased availability of affordable rented accommodation increases the flexibility of the labour market. Other things being equal, with a flexible labour market, recessions are less deep and recovery starts sooner than when the labour market is rigid and less flexible.

e This is an impressive answer that reaches Level 5. The candidate displays the skill of evaluation early in her answer, and there is also sufficient analysis to merit achieving the highest grade. She could have scored a few more marks by explaining in rather greater detail why unemployment might change for reasons other than those relating to the housing market. However, this is a quibble; the question requires discussion of the links between housing and unemployment rather than a detailed explanation and analysis of all the possible types or causes of unemployment.

13/15 marks

Scored 32/40 80% = grade A

Question 4

The automobile and the environment

Total for this question: 40 marks

Study **Extracts A**, **B**, and **C**, and then answer **all** parts of the question which follows.

Extract A The free ride is over for the automobile

The car is no ordinary consumer good. After a house, it is usually the most expensive thing ordinary people own. It is often charged with a good deal of emotion. Many people can recite the date they passed their driving test and they will fondly remember the first car they owned. Cars not only deliver freedom to go where you like, whenever you want; they can also be fun to look at and fun to drive. The question is whether the freedom and mobility they brought to a world of 2 billion people will still be available in a world rapidly heading for 10 billion.

The product that has so strongly shaped the urban world most of us live in, and brought such wealth and such pleasure, is now seen as an appalling threat to the environment: a blessing turned into a curse. Already cars and other vehicles are seen as the worst polluters of urban areas, the biggest producers of carbon dioxide and the chief suspect in global warming. They are also responsible for another ever-worsening negative externality: congestion.

Source: adapted from an article in *The Economist*, 22 June 1996.

Extract B Real changes in UK transport costs

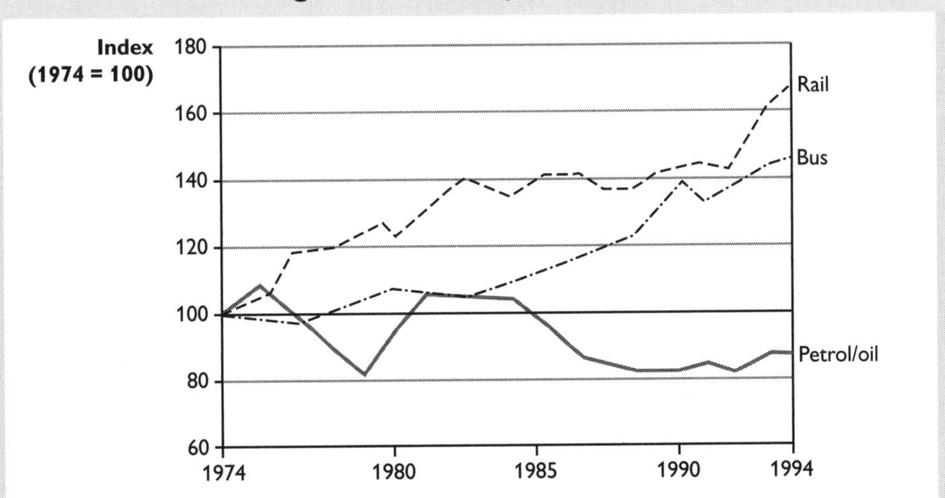

Source: *Indicators of Sustainable Development,* The Department of the Environment, 1996.

Extract C AA warns against green taxes

With car ownership expected to grow by a third over the next 20 years, the AA warned yesterday that the imposition of environmental taxes on motoring would reduce the quality of life for many groups, including women, the young and pensioners. The large rises in motoring costs would mean that many poorer families would have to make difficult choices — run an older car, or cut back on other parts of the family budget. Older cars, the AA claimed, were more damaging for the environment. The government could introduce road pricing as an alternative to taxation, but this would probably be more effective in reducing congestion rather than pollution.

Source: adapted from the *Financial Times*, 12 December 1996.

(a) What is meant by the term 'negative externality' (Extract A, line 13)? (3 marks)

(b) Compare the changes in UK transport costs between 1974 and 1994 which are shown in Extract B. (4 marks)

(c) Explain why the real change in the cost of motoring (shown by the data on petrol/oil in Extract B) differed from the real change in the cost of public transport. (8 marks)

(d) With the help of a diagram, explain how taxation may reduce negative externalities produced by the use of automobiles. (10 marks)

(e) In 2000 there were significant protests by vehicle owners about the level of taxation imposed on motorists. Do you agree that the government should use road pricing rather than taxation to deal with the adverse environmental effects of the motor car? Justify your reasoning. (15 marks)

■ ■ ■

Candidate's answer

(a) The defining characteristic of an externality is that it is delivered and received outside the market. It is the 'spin-off' effect of an economic activity, the benefit or cost being received by 'third parties'. A negative externality such as pollution and congestion is an external cost or 'bad' dumped on others.

e The candidate obviously has a good understanding of externalities, and writes more than enough to earn full marks. **3/3 marks**

(b) The real price or cost of bus and rail transport grew steadily over the period, with rail growing more than bus travel. By contrast the real price of petrol/oil (i.e. private motor transport) fell a little over the period, though it rose on two occasions before falling again. Overall, rail travel was twice as expensive as private motoring by 1994.

e The candidate picks up 2 of the available 4 marks for his first two sentences. However this is a rather generous mark because he shows no understanding of the fact that the data are in the form of index numbers. Because all three data series are based on 1974 = 100, it is impossible to conclude that rail travel was twice as expensive as private motoring in 1994. In any case, private motoring involves costs other than petrol/oil, e.g. motoring taxes. **2/4 marks**

(c) The reason why the cost of public transport rose by more than the cost of private motoring is because over the whole period, the prices charged for rail and bus rose by more than the rate of general inflation (measured, for example, by the RPI), while the price of petrol rose by less than the rate of general inflation. The latter means that the real cost of motoring actually fell over the whole period.

While the candidate shows a good understanding of statistical data, he fails to earn more than 4 of the 8 marks available because he does not provide a possible *economic* explanation beyond relating the data to the general rate of inflation. Candidates are not expected to possess knowledge of the UK economy going back beyond ten years. As the data in Extract B go back longer than this, any plausible explanation can gain marks: for example, in terms of different taxes levied on different forms of transport, or changes in productive efficiency amongst the different forms of transport. In fact, part of the explanation stems from the fact that, in real terms, oil prices peaked in 1974 just after the price of crude oil had been raised several hundred per cent by OPEC in the first oil crisis. In later years, tax increases imposed on petrol were insufficient to offset the fall in the real price of crude oil, so over the period petrol prices fell in real terms. Meanwhile the reduction or removal of government subsidies caused public transport prices to rise in real terms. **4/8 marks**

(d) The main way in which taxation can reduce the negative externalities of pollution and congestion resulting from automobiles is if taxes are imposed on motor car *use* rather than car *ownership* — unless a tax on ownership was set at such a high level that it deterred ownership significantly and hence also significantly reduced car use! The best way to do this is to tax fuel: petrol and diesel fuel.

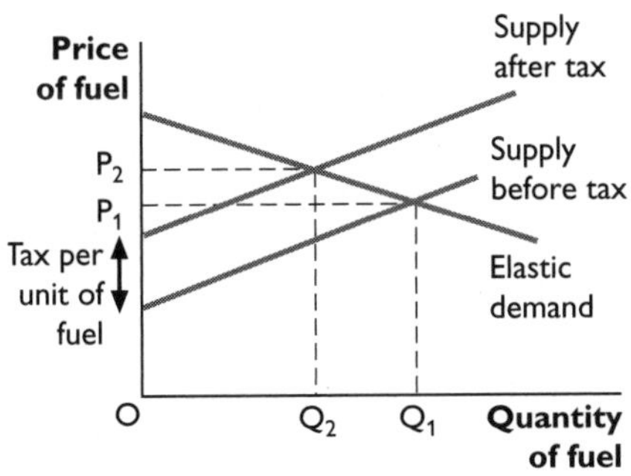

Elastic demand

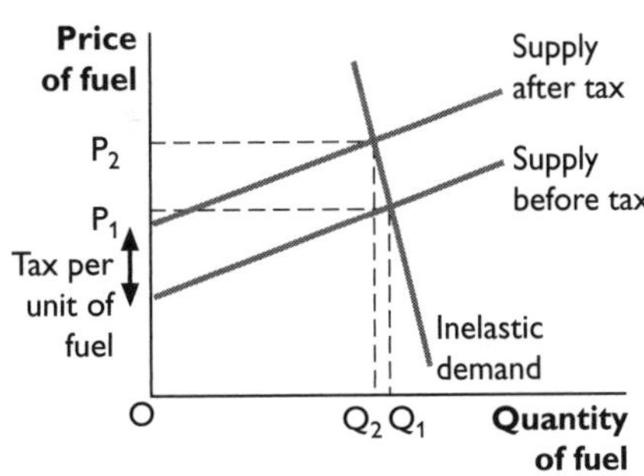

Inelastic demand

However, as my diagram shows, the effectiveness of a fuel tax depends on the elasticity of demand for fuel (and hence for car use), as well as on how high the tax is. I have drawn highly elastic and highly inelastic demand curves respectively in the left-hand and right-hand panels of the diagram. The graphs clearly show that when the same tax is imposed, there is a more than proportionate fall in demand for motor fuel when demand is elastic, but a less than proportionate fall when demand is inelastic.

This is an excellent answer that earns all 10 marks. No criticism can be made of the answer, but there is an extra possible point to make. The candidate might have stated that much of the taxation imposed on motorists is based on the *polluter must pay* principle. The more the motorist pollutes (and/or causes congestion), the greater the tax the motorist must pay. This does two things. First, the tax imitates the *incentive function of prices*, i.e. the tax creates the incentive to economise in the use of fuel and motor cars. Second, by thrusting the cost of pollution (and/or congestion) back on the motorist who causes it, the tax *internalises the externality*.

10/10 marks

(e) Road pricing and taxation (provided it taxes car use rather than car ownership) have similar advantages. In the absence of road pricing or taxation, motorists consider only the private costs they incur, primarily the cost of fuel and wear and tear to the vehicle. Because the pollution and congestion they generate are mostly external costs, motorists don't take them into account when deciding whether or not to use their cars. Motoring thus becomes under-priced compared to other forms of travel, particularly to public transport, leading to over-use of motor vehicles and roads.

Both road pricing and taxation can, in principle, correct this situation. Both can 'internalise the externality', i.e. force the cost of the externality back on the motorist responsible for causing it. But road congestion occurs almost exclusively in built-up areas and vehicle pollution is also worst in such areas. The disadvantage of raising petrol tax to try to reduce congestion is that, for this purpose, it is much too blunt an instrument. By this I mean that it hits rural motorists driving, say, 30 miles to work on uncongested roads much more than it hits my mother driving 5 miles each day on a school run taking my sister to school but also contributing significantly to congestion.

But whereas road pricing has the advantage over fuel taxation of reducing or punishing those who cause congestion, the situation is probably reversed for pollution. Virtually *all* motorists emit pollution, whereas only *some* cause congestion. Road pricing is best used selectively on roads prone to congestion, for example during rush hours but not at night. By contrast, taxation is best used to deter and punish emission of pollutants by all motorists. It can be used selectively, but in a different way to road pricing, for example by taxing owners of large or 'dirty' vehicles much more than small and 'clean' vehicles.

My conclusion therefore is that taxation and road pricing should not be viewed as alternatives or as substitutes for each other, but as complementary policies, along with other policies such as improving public transport, developing new and much cleaner propulsion technologies such as electric cars, etc.

The candidate rounds off the examination with another excellent, thoughtful and knowledgeable answer, which achieves full marks. He includes just the right combination of analysis and evaluation in the answer, fully obeying the instruction to 'justify his reasoning'.

15/15 marks

Scored 34/40 85% = grade A

Valuing the environment

Total for this question: 40 marks

Study **Extracts A**, **B** and **C**, and then answer **all** parts of the question which follows.

Extract A Placing a value on the environment

The natural environment provides us with many economic resources which we consume as 'free' goods. But because they are free, people tend to undervalue the services that the environment provides. Professor David Pearce argues that to treat these environmental resources as if they had no value is seriously to risk overusing the resource. He quotes the example of the ozone layer. Because the ozone layer has been treated as a free resource, people have lacked the incentive to protect it. If no price is charged, the incentive function of prices cannot operate.

Simple supply and demand analysis tells us that when a good or service is provided free, more of it will be demanded than would be the case if a positive price were charged. However, the greater level of demand is unlikely to bear any relation to the ability of the natural environment to meet the demand. But resources and environments do serve economic functions and have a positive value. We should question the axiom of economics that anything that does not have to be paid for has no monetary value — even if its absence would cause the most horrendous problems. People have to be made aware that they are fundamentally dependent on ecosystems. It's either that — or wait until nature sends its own form of bailiff around to collect the unpaid debts. The environment may seem to be giving us a free lunch, but the bill may be on the way. Eventually we shall have to pay and the payment will be very heavy indeed.

Source: adapted from *The Independent*, 6 January 1998.

Extract B The 'unpaid bills' of the 'real service economy': an estimate of the value of some of the services provided 'free' in 1997 to the world economy by the environment

CO_2 sequestration	$135 bn	Host plant resistance (forest)	$6 bn
Waste disposal	$760 bn	Perennial grains (potential)	$170 bn
Soil formation	$25 bn	Pollination	$200 bn
Nitrogen fixation	$90 bn	Fishing	$60 bn
Hunting	$25 bn	Seafood	$82 bn
Crop breeding (genetics)	$115 bn	Other wild foods	$180 bn
Livestock breeding (genetics)	$40 bn	Pharmaceuticals from plants	$84 bn
Biocontrol of pests (crops)	$100 bn	Wood products	$84 bn
Biocontrol of pests (forests)	$60 bn	Ecotourism	$500 bn

Source: adapted from *The Independent*, 6 January 1998.

Extract C How much is the natural world really worth?

If you're studying its rain forests, for example, should their value be estimated in terms of the wood they contain? Or should it also include the indigenous animal and plant species which are known to contain useful pharmaceuticals? Or, should we put a value on rain forests based on their ability to absorb atmospheric carbon, and hence mitigate the greenhouse effect?

Increasingly, earth scientists are trying to put serious values on what our environment provides us with — a 24-hour-a-day, seven-day-a-week service economy that never shuts down or takes a holiday. 'If all the planet's biota, all the plants and animals and micro-organisms, sent a bill for their 1997 services, the total would be $2.9 trillion', says Professor David Pimental of the Ecology Department at Cornell University in the USA. By Professor Pimental's calculations (shown in Extract B), the USA's share of that bill would be $319 billion. Bearing in mind that US gross domestic product was around $6.8 trillion, it can be seen that the ecosystem is a significant, yet unrewarded, part of any economy.

If 'the ecosystem' were in fact a trading partner which charged — for air, water, animal breeding, seafood, hunting and so on — the laws of supply and demand might rapidly put the USA into deficit. 'When you compare our spending to preserve biodiversity to the benefits we reap, we're really getting a bargain', says Professor Pimental.

Source: adapted from an article by Charles Arthur in *The Independent*, 6 January 1998.

(a) With the use of an example, explain the meaning of the term 'free good' (Extract A, line 2). (3 marks)

(b) What is the incentive function of prices (Extract A, line 7)? (4 marks)

(c) Extract B shows an estimate of the value of some of the services provided 'free' in 1997 to the world economy by the environment. Making use of the information in Extract C, explain why it might be difficult to place a monetary value on TWO of the items listed in the table. (8 marks)

(d) With the help of a diagram, explain the statement 'when a good or service is provided free, more of it will be demanded than would be the case if a positive price were charged' (Extract A, lines 8–10). (10 marks)

(e) According to lines 17–19 of Extract A, the environment may seem to be giving us a free lunch, but eventually we shall all have to pay heavily. To what extent do you agree with this view? Justify your reasoning. (15 marks)

■ ■ ■

Candidate's answer

(a) A free good is the same thing as a public good such as national defence, or a merit good such as state education, both of which the government provides free.

e This answer earns no marks because the candidate has confused a genuine *free good* with a *good that happens to be free*, in the sense that although it is made available to consumers at zero price, scarce resources are used up, and costs of production are incurred, in its provision. A genuine free good is one that is available in unlimited quantity at zero cost of production. There is unlimited supply, no scarcity and no opportunity cost in supply. The air we breathe is an example, although absolutely clean or pure air is seldom a free good. **0/3 marks**

(b) Prices perform three main functions in the economy, known as the signalling, incentive and rationing functions. The information signalled by the good's price (and by relative prices of other goods) creates incentives for consumers and firms to behave in particular ways. For a consumer, information about price, along with other information about quality, enables the good to be compared to other goods to see if it is worth buying. For a firm, the information indicates whether profits can be made by producing and selling the good. This is the incentive function of prices.

This is a good answer that earns full marks. The candidate obviously knows and understands the three functions of prices set out in the AS Economics specification, and provides a confident and clear explanation of the incentive function.

4/4 marks

(c) The examples I have selected from Extract B are CO_2 sequestration and crop breeding (genetics). I believe that the former relates to the role of trees, and the tropical rain forests in particular, in acting as a 'sink' by absorbing carbon dioxide (CO_2) from the atmosphere. Extract B calculates the monetary value of CO_2 sequestration in 1997 at $135 billion. Likewise the value of crop breeding in 1997 was calculated to be $115 billion. I take this to mean the improvements in crops and animals that occurred in 1997 as a result of genetic research from which all farmers (and consumers) may benefit in future years.

After a good start, the candidate does not develop the economics of his answer sufficiently to earn full marks. In particular, he fails to address the key issue of the question: namely, why it is difficult to place a *monetary value* on the benefits of CO_2 sequestration and crop and animal breeding. This is a disguised question on positive (environmental) externalities. The central issue is that forests and the genetic improvement of crops and animals are producing positive externalities from which other people benefit for free. Because there is no market in these positive externalities, no price is charged for the benefits and it is difficult to give them a monetary value. However, the advent of genetically modified crops may change this; companies such as Monsanto are trying to patent and charge for genetic improvements. **3/8 marks**

(d) The demand curve for a good shows the quantities of the good that all the consumers in the market are prepared to buy at different possible prices. Economists assume that the demand curve for most goods slopes downward from left to right, like the one I have drawn below. If this is the case, then more is demanded at low prices than at high prices.

Suppose the price in the market is P_1. As my diagram shows, consumers demand quantity Q_1 at this price. But if the good was made available free (zero price), the

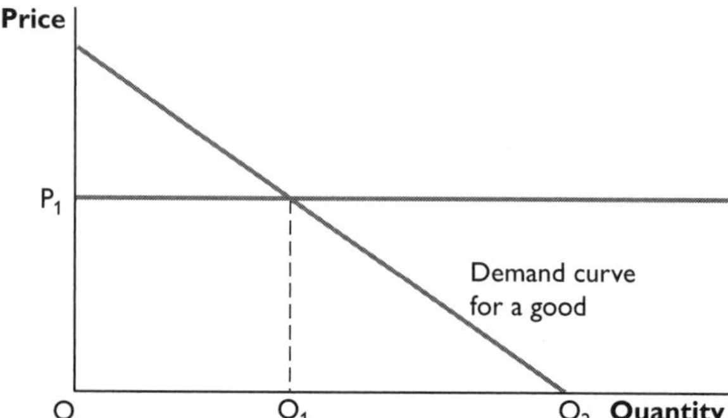

quantity demanded would be Q_2. In virtually every market, however, goods are not available free. Most goods command a price because *supply* is limited in relation to *demand*. It is useful also to note that when the demand curve is vertical (i.e. completely inelastic), the same amount is demanded at all prices — including zero price.

This time the candidate has focused fully on the question and, as a consequence, earned full marks. This answer could not really be improved. **8/8 marks**

(e) There is a saying in economics: 'there is no such thing as a free lunch'. What this means is that things that appear to be free are not in fact free. In my answer to question (a), I defined a free good as a public good. But a public good such as national defence is not in fact free. As its provision uses up scarce resources, it has an opportunity cost. Any good which appears to be free has an opportunity cost, so it is not free. Somebody has to pay for the food in my lunch, even if I am getting it free in the sense that I am not paying for it.

So when the environment provides us with apparently free goods such as a beautiful view, there is an opportunity cost. It is not free because the government or owners of land are using up scarce resources to maintain the quality of the landscape so as to maintain the view that we are enjoying.

This a reasonable answer, as far as it goes, but unfortunately it does not go far enough. In his answer to question (a), the candidate wrongly defined a free good as a public good. He refers back to his earlier answer when answering this question, but in this case the point he makes is relevant because a public good very definitely does have an opportunity cost. As he rightly concludes, somebody has to pay for a public good, even though it is provided apparently free to those who benefit from it.

However, the answer is a Level 3 answer (7–9 marks) rather than a Level 4 answer (10–12 marks). To earn a higher mark he would have to analyse the time aspect of the question. The key words in the question are 'eventually we shall all have to pay heavily'. This question is about what economists call *inter-temporal choice*, i.e. choice between something now and something in the future. To reach Level 4, there must be some analysis of this choice, while to reach Level 5 there must then be some evaluation of the significance of the choice. **7/15 marks**

Scored 22/40 55% = grade C

Global warming

Total for this question: 40 marks

Study **Extracts A**, **B** and **C**, and then answer **all** parts of the question which follows.

Extract A How to reduce CO_2 emissions

CO_2 emissions result from burning non-renewable natural resources, coal and oil. The market system is unlikely to reduce CO_2 emissions. The need arises, therefore, for governments to intervene to ensure that the polluter covers the costs that would otherwise be incurred by the rest of society. This is known as the 'polluter must pay' principle. Most deforestation takes place in developing countries, but it is clear that the industrialised countries that are largely responsible for CO_2 emissions have a considerable interest in preserving forests, 60% of which are in developing countries. A complementary policy would be to introduce a carbon tax which would be levied on the carbon content of fossil fuels to reduce CO_2 emissions.

Source: adapted from an article in *The British Economic Survey*, autumn 1992.

Extract B The economics of global warming

Global warming arises from the 'greenhouse effect', whereby the accumulation of certain gases in the earth's atmosphere allows radiation from the sun to enter the earth's atmosphere, but prevents some of the radiation from escaping back out of the atmosphere. The principal greenhouse gases involved are carbon dioxide (CO_2), CFCs, methane and nitrous oxide. Carbon dioxide contributes to 50% of global warming. CO_2 emissions are associated with the burning of fossil fuels and also with deforestation, since forests are a natural 'sink' for CO_2.

Some of the basic issues associated with global warming are:

(1) There are two broad policy choices: on the one hand, we could do nothing to reduce emissions and just adapt to higher temperatures; on the other hand, we could try to slow the accumulation of gases in the atmosphere by cutting back on emissions of greenhouse gases.

(2) If we decide to reduce emissions, by how much should we try to reduce them?

(3) There are different ways of reducing emissions of greenhouse gases: for example, we could switch the mix of fuels we use away from coal, oil and gas towards renewable sources or nuclear power; we could try to reduce the amount of energy we consume; or we could plant trees to lock in more CO_2. What mix of such methods should we use?

(4) Whatever mix we decide upon, what policy instruments should we use to bring it about?

Source: adapted from an article in *The Economic Review*, November 1991.

Extract C Sources of CO_2 emissions by industry and country type

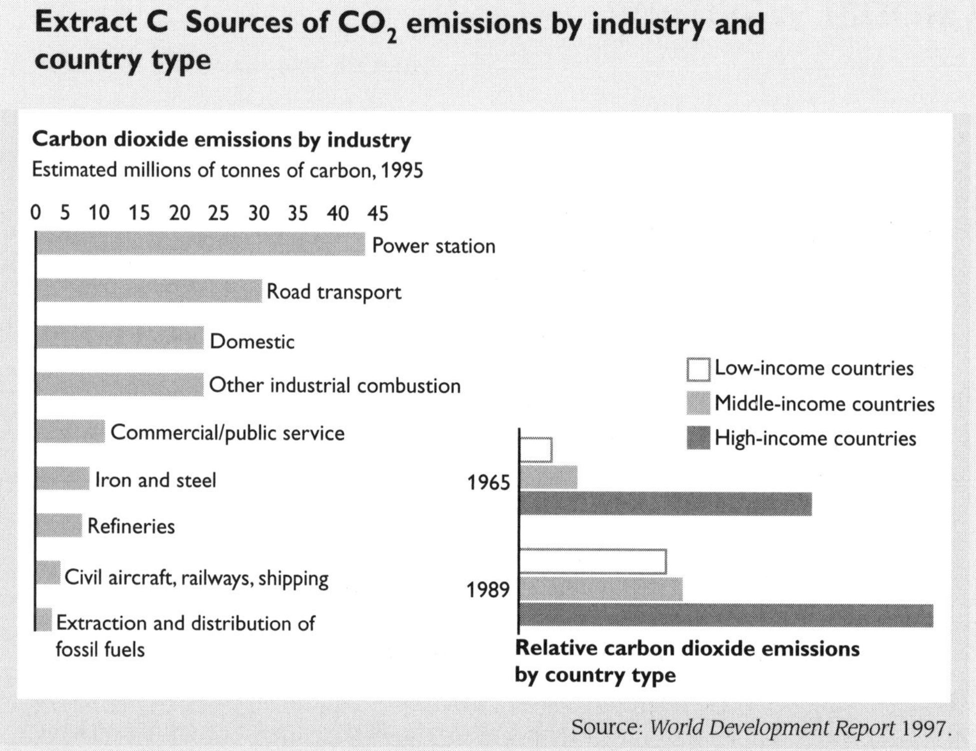

Source: *World Development Report* 1997.

(a) With the use of an example, explain the meaning of the term 'non-renewable natural resources' (Extract A, line 1). (3 marks)

(b) Explain why the emission of greenhouse gases leads to market failure. (4 marks)

(c) In the light of the information in Extracts A and C, explain one policy initiative (other than a carbon tax) which might reduce or mitigate the effect of CO_2 emissions. (8 marks)

(d) With the help of a diagram, illustrate how a carbon tax, based on the 'polluter must pay' principle, might reduce emissions of CO_2. (10 marks)

(e) Extract B states that one policy option is to do nothing to reduce global warming, but to adapt to live with the consequences. Identify and evaluate the costs and benefits of such an approach. (15 marks)

■ ■ ■

Candidate's answer

(a) A resource is a factor of production that is used in production. A natural resource occurs naturally as a result of geological, biological and/or climatic processes, e.g. the fertility of the soil or mineral deposits. A non-renewable natural resource is one that becomes depleted as it is used. Examples are fossil fuels such as coal and oil, and metals such as copper.

The candidate has made absolutely sure she earns full marks by defining in sequence the three key words in the question — resource, natural and non-renewable — and by providing, as required, an accurate example. **3/3 marks**

(b) The emission of greenhouse gases such as CO_2 leads to market failure because the gases provide examples of negative externalities. Negative externalities cause markets to fail because the effects they produce are undesirable, for example causing buildings to crumble, trees to suffer stunted growth and fish to die. Greenhouse gases cause markets to fail because they lead to global warming, worse weather and higher sea levels and flooding.

After the quality of the answer to the first part of the question, this answer is disappointing. The candidate has fallen into the trap of describing some of the adverse and perhaps colourful effects of negative externalities without explaining the *economics* of why negative externalities lead to market failure. She could explain that because there is no market in a negative externality (i.e. a 'missing market'), the economic agents responsible for greenhouse gas emission have no incentive to produce lower levels of the gases. An allocatively inefficient amount is produced, both of the externality and of the good for which the externality is a spin-off. She might also argue that motorists and others responsible for greenhouse gases pay too little for fossil fuels. This leads to over-use of motor vehicles and fuel, since part of the true or real cost of motoring — the cost of carbon pollution dumped into the atmosphere — is not borne by motorists. **1/4 marks**

(c) Extract C shows that power stations that burn fossil fuels (mostly coal) are the most important single source of CO_2 emissions, followed by road transport. It also shows, first, that emissions have been growing, and, second, that high-income countries emit more CO_2 than middle- and low-income countries combined.

One policy option that might reduce emissions by power stations and by major polluters in manufacturing industry is a market in tradable permits to pollute. Such a scheme was introduced for American power stations in the early 1990s, and has been quite successful. The Kyoto conference on global warming that took place in the late 1990s discussed the introduction of a global variation on this theme in which rich countries would buy 'spare' emission permits from poor countries, paying for them in hard currency that would benefit the poor countries.

Again this answer disappoints — all the more so because it started well. The candidate made use of the information in Extract C, but did not make use of the stimulus material in Extract A. The extract made reference to preserving forests which, by acting as carbon 'sinks' absorbing carbon from the atmosphere, mitigate the effects of carbon dioxide emissions. Although the candidate structured her answer around another relevant policy option, namely tradable markets in permits to pollute, in principle she could still have picked up full marks, but only if she had obeyed the key instruction to *explain* how permits to pollute might achieve carbon dioxide reduction. Pollution permits create market-related incentives for power stations to reduce pollution. Power stations that can reduce pollution by more than

the law requires can make money by selling their 'spare' pollution permits to power stations that find it difficult to comply with the law. The latter power stations have an incentive to clean up their act to avoid the cost of buying the extra pollution permits they need to pollute legally. Her answer only skirted around this explanation — hence the relatively low mark. **3/8 marks**

(d) The diagram I have drawn below shows how a pollution tax might reduce emissions of CO_2.

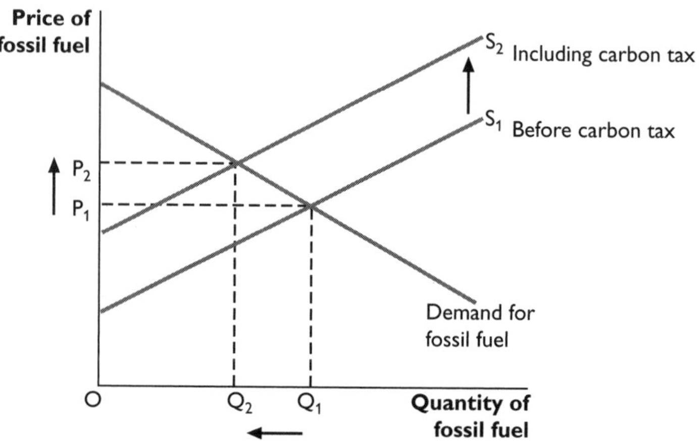

Before the pollution tax is imposed, the price of a fossil fuel such as petrol is P_1 and the quantity that motorists purchase is Q_1. As my diagram shows, a pollution tax shifts the supply curve of fossil fuel upwards (from S_1 to S_2). A higher price (P_2) results, which creates the incentive for motorists to economise and use less fossil fuel (Q_2 rather than Q_1). Providing that the size of the carbon tax fully reflects the cost of the negative externality emitted by motorists, the pollution tax 'internalises the externality', i.e. imposes the cost of the externality back on to those responsible for producing the externality. Hence the polluter pays.

e After the wobble in the answer to the previous question, the candidate is back on form with this answer. She addresses the question at all times, and her written answer and diagram nicely complement each other. As a result, she earns full marks. **10/10 marks**

(e) Perhaps the main reason why more effort should be spent learning to live with the consequences of global warming stems from the likely fact that global warming cannot be stopped or reversed. The best we can hope for is merely to slow down the process of global warming. As I write, we are already living with the consequences in Britain. The climate is becoming stormier and wetter, leading to flooding. Flooding will become worse as sea level rises. Other parts of the world are suffering the opposite problems of drought and desertification.

Trying to stop global warming completely is a little like whistling in the wind. I say this because as GDP and living standards rise across the world, demand for cars and electricity rises. This is because they are 'normal goods', the demand for which increases with income — but, as Extract C shows, they are also the big producers of global warming gases. Who are we, the citizens of the developed world who already enjoy high living standards partly made possible by burning fossil fuels, to stop poor people in developing countries from trying to raise their living standards? We are only being hypocritical if we ask them to stop cutting down and burning tropical rain forests, when in previous centuries we cut down our own forests.

But a balance has to be struck. It is not a choice of one or the other. Governments and policy makers must make every effort to slow down and *eventually* reverse global warming. They can do this by encouraging conservation, tree planting, new technologies and alternative lifestyles. But at the same time they must take practical steps to ameliorate the consequences. These must include stopping house building on flood plains, building flood barriers and setting up funds to help people who, through no fault of their own, have their homes or livelihoods threatened by the effects of global warming.

e This answer reaches Level 4 because it focuses on the question and contains some evaluation and analysis. However, the answer becomes a little woolly when the candidate rather contradicts herself. After arguing that it is best to learn to live with the consequences of global warming because it is impossible to stop or reverse the process, she later argues that governments should try to reverse global warming. Because of this inconsistency, and the lack of sufficient development of her analysis, she earns a mark of 10 at the bottom of the Level 4 band (10–12).

10/15 marks

Scored 27/40 67% = grade B

The economics of sport

Total for this question: 40 marks

Study **Extracts A**, **B** and **C**, and then answer **all** parts of the question which follows.

Extract A Sport as a commodity

It is possible to classify sport under three headings. First, sport is a non-durable consumer good: that is, the benefit that matters to the consumer is generated at the time of consumption. Most sports spectating fits within this category of consumer demand. Each spectator weighs up the potential enjoyment from watching a sport and makes a judgement on whether this is worth more or less than the admission price and/or the time spent watching the event. Equally, most playing of sport is of this non-durable consumption type: people take part because they enjoy it and derive more satisfaction than it costs them to take part.

Participation in sport, however, can generate benefits that are not immediate. If taking part in sport results in the person being physically in better shape, this is a durable consumption good, since the benefits build up over time. Thirdly, sport can possess the characteristic of a capital good. If sport makes a person fitter and healthier, then this may lead to a 'pay-off' in terms of increased productivity in the labour market and higher labour market income.

Many sports are also normal goods, some with an income elasticity of demand greater than +1. Participation in these sports increases when the economy is doing well, but falls when the economy is in recession. Other sports may, however, be inferior goods.

Extract B Estimates of cross elasticity of demand between similar leisure facilities

Various attempts have been made to estimate the cross elasticity of demand between apparently similar leisure facilities located fairly close to each other. Because they are substitutes, economic theory would suggest that the cross elasticity of demand for the facilities offered by one sports centre with respect to a change in the price of similar facilities at a nearby sports centre should be positive. However, a research project which studied pricing at Scottish sports centres in 1993 did not produce this result.

The project studied two swimming pools that are 4 miles apart. One of the pools experimented with free use for casual swimmers. The other pool offered a greater range of activities and higher-quality swimming facilities. The free use experiment had a negligible effect on the demand for the other pool, which had constant visit numbers despite the free entry competition. Formally, the cross-price elasticity of demand was zero and not what economic theory might have led us to expect.

Extract C Selected statistics of prices charged and usage of three sports centres

	Average % price change	% change in usage (in year following price change)	% change in revenue (in year following price change)	Price elasticity of demand
Sports Centre 1	+13	–3	+19	–0.23
Sports Centre 2	+70	–37	+11	—
Sports Centre 3	+15	+134	+120	+8.9

Source: all items adapted from Chris Gratton and Peter Taylor, *The Economics of Sport and Recreation* (E. and F. N. Spon, 2000).

(a) What is meant by the term 'capital good' (Extract A, line 12)? (3 marks)

(b) Explain the significance of a sport having an income elasticity of demand greater than +1 (Extract A, lines 15–16). (4 marks)

(c) Calculate the price elasticity of demand for Sports Centre 2 shown in Extract C, and discuss the implications of this elasticity for the Sports Centre's pricing policy. (8 marks)

(d) Explain the meaning of cross elasticity of demand and why the cross elasticities estimated for the two sports centres that are mentioned in Extract B turned out to be not what economic theory might have led us to expect. (10 marks)

(e) Evaluate the case for and against charging commercial prices for the use of sports centres, rather than allowing people to use them free or at reduced prices, subsidised by the government. (15 marks)

■ ■ ■

Candidate's answer

(a) Unlike a service, which is intangible, a good is tangible, i.e. it has a definite substance. A capital good is long-lasting. It delivers a continuing stream of useful services.

> This answer only earns 1 of the 3 available marks — for defining a good. It is impossible to award more marks because the candidate shows no understanding of the term *capital*. A capital good, such as a machine, is a good that is used to produce other goods or services. Businesses rather than consumers buy capital goods. Many capital goods are durable, delivering a continuing stream of services, but as this is irrelevant to the question, no more marks can be awarded. **1/3 marks**

(b) If a sport has an income elasticity of demand greater than +1, it means that when income increases, demand for the sport increases at a faster proportionate rate. The sport would be a luxury good or a superior good. Water-skiing might be an example. Because water-skiing lessons and equipment are very expensive, rich rather than poor people tend to water-ski.

This answer shows good understanding. To earn the fourth mark, the candidate needed to focus a little more on the word *significance*: for example, by explaining that demand for water-skiing might increase more than proportionately when national income rises, but fall more than proportionately when the economy enters a recession and incomes fall. **3/4 marks**

(c) I am using the following formula to calculate the price elasticity of demand for Sports Centre 2:

$$\text{elasticity} = \frac{\text{\% change in demand for Sports Centre 2}}{\text{\% change in price charged}} = \frac{-37\%}{+70\%} = -0.53$$

This means that demand is inelastic. The implication is that an increase in price will lead to a less than proportionate fall in demand.

This is an answer of two halves: the first part is excellent but the candidate fails to get to grips with the second part of the question. Her elasticity calculation was absolutely correct, but even if the candidate had made an arithmetical error, she would still have picked up some of the 4 available marks. This is because she included the correct formula in her answer and displayed the correct method. It is always a good idea to show how you are performing calculations. However, the rest of the answer disappoints. To earn a further 4 marks the candidate needs to mention two implications of the elasticity statistic she has calculated. She might explain that when demand is inelastic, customers are less sensitive to price changes, and that revenue increases (according to the table in Extract C by 11%) following a price increase. The candidate's answer only earns 1 of the 4 marks available for this half of the question. **5/8 marks**

(d) Cross elasticity of demand measures the proportionate change in the demand for one good, following a change in the price of another good. With regard to the example quoted in Extract B, the following formula would be used to calculate the cross elasticity of demand between the two swimming pools:

$$\text{cross elasticity of demand for pool A} = \frac{\text{\% change in demand for pool A}}{\text{\% change in price charged by pool B}}$$

As Extract B states, we usually expect the cross elasticity of demand between two substitutes to be positive. When the price of one of the goods increases, consumers demand more of the substitute good that has become relatively cheaper. There are a number of possible reasons why the cross elasticity of demand between the two swimming pools in Extract B was zero rather than positive. First, the research might have been flawed, resulting in an inaccurate elasticity calculation. Second, and related to this, other factors that influence demand such as advertising might have been shifting demand curves for the two pools during the course of the study. The third explanation, and in my opinion the most likely, is that because of the different quality of the two pools, they were not regarded as substitutes by customers and potential customers. And although 4 miles is not a great distance, it might be sufficient for each pool to have its own 'catchment area'.

This is an excellent answer that earns full marks. As in her previous answer, the candidate has shown an accurate understanding of the elasticity concept in the question. In this instance, however, she has written a developed and plausible explanation that fully answers the second part of the question. **10/10 marks**

(e) I am going to answer this question by arguing that sports centres are merit goods. When one person consumes a merit good, the social benefits enjoyed by the whole community are greater than the private benefits derived by the individual consumer. Positive externalities are produced which benefit the whole community.

I think for sports centres, two main positive externalities result, namely public health benefits and a reduction in crime. Obviously individuals who use sports centres become fitter and healthier, but the whole community also benefits. A healthier population should mean lower taxation, as fit and healthy people tend to work and there are fewer unhealthy people to be a burden on the taxpayer. Also, if young people use sports centres, there will be fewer aimless people wandering the streets being tempted into crime.

However, these external benefits are only fully realised when access to sports centres is free. When prices are charged, many people — especially the poor — are priced out of their use. Hence the case for providing free sports centres, financed out of taxation. It increases the quality of life of poorer people in society.

However there are counter-arguments. First, when goods or services are provided free, consumers tend to undervalue them. Second, the quality of facilities provided by commercially run sports centres often tends to be higher than those provided by those run by local authorities. Third, there is an opportunity cost, namely the other useful goods and services that taxpayers' money could provide if it wasn't used to provide free sports centres.

This answer starts off well, focusing immediately on the main issue candidates are expected to discuss: whether sports centres are a merit good. Indeed, the 'case against charging' commercial prices for the use of sports centres is very well presented. Unfortunately, the 'case for charging' is presented in truncated form. Each of the points made, though valid, needs more explanation and development. But to reach Level 5 (13–15 marks), some evaluation of the relative strength of the cases for and against is required. There is no such evaluation in this answer. Because the candidate includes relevant analysis when making the 'case against charging' and at least mentions relevant arguments for charging, overall the answer reaches mid-Level 4. **11/15 marks**

Scored 30/40 75% = grade B

The economics of tourism

Total for this question: 40 marks

Study **Extracts A**, **B** and **C**, and then answer **all** parts of the question which follows.

Extract A Tourism as a product

As a product, tourism presents a unique combination of characteristics. Because much of the output of tourism comprises services rather than goods, it is impossible to separate production and consumption. For example, a seat on a particular flight, a night's stay at a particular hotel on a particular night, entry to a tourist attraction on a particular day or a place on a boat trip to a beach, cannot be stored. If they are not consumed when they are produced, that day's production will be lost for ever. Thus it is not possible for airlines to store empty seats on an aeroplane for future use.

Tourism in most parts of the world is highly seasonal. The peak season will depend on the type of tourism, e.g. a beach or skiing holiday, and this in turn will be affected by the weather. Other types of tourism will be linked to particular events, such as the Olympic Games or a religious festival.

A further feature of tourism is that tourists frequently share use of a tourist amenity with local residents, which can be a potential source of conflict. For example, tourists use large quantities of water for showers and baths, and in countries where water is scarce, this can cause anger amongst both farmers and local residents, who are deprived of access to their 'own' water supply as it has been diverted to tourist use.

Tourist destinations are perishable in a second sense. Fashions and hence tastes change or resorts can be spoilt if they are overdeveloped. This can lead to a decline in visitors to particular destinations.

Extract B The impact of F$1,000 tourist expenditure on Fiji balance of payments

		F$
Tourist expenditure		1,000.0
Import requirements		
Direct	120.8	
Indirect	115.3	
		–236.1
Net effect on balance of payments		763.9
Induced imports	326.3	–326.3
Net impact after induced effects		437.6
Repatriated income	53.0	–53.0
Net impact after repatriated income		384.6

Extract C The economic impact of tourism

Spending by tourists has a number of beneficial effects, including a multiplier effect on the local economy. Tourists spend directly on hotels, restaurants, theme parks and souvenirs. There is also an indirect effect on expenditure and goods related to tourism, such as construction of hotels and amenities, water supplies and other services. This induced effect generates non-tourist spending by local residents.

According to Extract B, the tourist expenditure multiplier in Fiji is 1.38. For every thousand Fijian dollars spent by tourists, the island's economy is stimulated by a further 384.6 dollars worth of economic activity. There are two reasons why the multiplier effect resulting from tourist spending is quite small. First, tourism is often concentrated in small countries or regions that have to import many of the supplies needed from other countries or regions. Second, many tourist amenities are not owned locally, but by large multinational companies. Much of the profit is repatriated to the country in which the parent company is based.

Tourism obviously creates employment. However, over-dependence on tourism will leave a country or resort vulnerable to sudden changes in demand. Also, the work tends to be seasonal and often unskilled and low paid. Employment created in tourism also has an opportunity cost, measured by lost output in other industries.

Tourism is an important earner of foreign currency and it can provide a boost to government revenue, which is particularly welcome in poor countries where the local tax base is small. It also promotes the development of infrastructure such as airports, roads and telecommunications. But there are many external costs of tourism, including increased traffic congestion and pollution. Finally, the increased demand for land, housing and local products will cause inflation which adversely affects the local population.

Source: all items adapted from an article by Tony Westaway in *Developments in Economics*, Vol. 17 (Causeway Press, 2001).

(a) Explain the difference between a 'good' and a 'service' (Extract A, line 2). (3 marks)

(b) Lines 3–7 of Extract A state that much of the output of the tourist industry cannot be stored. Identify TWO problems this might pose for a tourist industry. (4 marks)

(c) Using Extracts B and C, explain the meaning of the 'tourist expenditure multiplier', and ONE implication for a tourist region or country of a small tourist expenditure multiplier. (8 marks)

(d) With the help of a diagram, explain how the prices charged by hotels for accommodation may vary between seasons at a beach resort. (10 marks)

(e) Do you agree that the economic advantages of tourism for a country such as Fiji exceed the disadvantages? Justify your answer. (15 marks)

Candidate's answer

(a) A good is tangible, i.e. it is a physical 'thing' such as a car or a loaf of bread. By contrast a service is for the most part intangible, such as the health care advice given by a doctor or the education provided by a teacher.

> This is an accurate answer that explains the two concepts concisely, and provides suitable examples. **3/3 marks**

(b) In the autumn of 2001 a terrorist outrage caused a massive drop in demand for air flights and hotel bookings. Airlines and hotel companies still had to pay many of their operating costs, but the cancelled bookings were lost for ever, yielding no revenue for the companies concerned. A number of airlines such as Swiss Air and Sabena went bankrupt and had to cease trading. Likewise one of the most famous restaurants in the City of Bath, where I live, went out of business because of a big drop in the number of American tourists visiting the city.

> The candidate makes good use of examples, but he needs to focus on the fact that, unlike goods, tourist services cannot be stored. Firms that manufacture or sell goods can also go bankrupt if business falls away. But, unlike services, goods can usually be stored and sold at a later date. Also he only identifies one problem; the question asks for two problems. **2/4 marks**

(c) The multiplier measures the relationship between a change in aggregate demand or expenditure in an economy and the resulting change in the level of national income or output. For example, if the size of the multiplier is 5, an increase in aggregate demand of £1 billion increases national income by £5 billion. The tourist expenditure multiplier is a special case of the multiplier, measuring the effect on national income resulting from an increase in expenditure by overseas tourists visiting a country.

Extracts B and C indicate that for Fiji, the tourist expenditure multiplier is 1.38. If correct, this indicates that when foreign tourists spend £1 million while visiting Fiji, the Fijian economy benefits by a further £380,000 as the effect of the spending ripples through the Fijian economy.

> This answer starts off very well. The candidate obviously has a good understanding of the multiplier process, which involves an initial increase in aggregate demand triggering multiple and successively smaller stages of income generation, with the sum of the stages being a multiple of the initial increase in demand. However, the answer fails to earn full marks because the candidate ignores a key instruction in the question: *to explain one implication* for a tourist region or country of a small tourist expenditure multiplier. One implication could be that the stimulus to the economy is quite limited, probably because a large part of the income received by the small country's tourist industry is spent on imports. Spending on imports stimulates other countries' income rather than that of the country that tourists are visiting. **6/8 marks**

(d) In my diagram, I have drawn a vertical supply curve to represent the inelastic supply curve of hotel accommodation which, at least in the short run, cannot increase. In the summer peak season, I have drawn the demand curve for accommodation in a position to the right of the winter off-peak demand curve. (I am assuming that peak demand is in the summer and off-peak demand in the winter. This is the case in Mediterranean beach resorts, but the seasonal demand might be different, for example, in the Caribbean.)

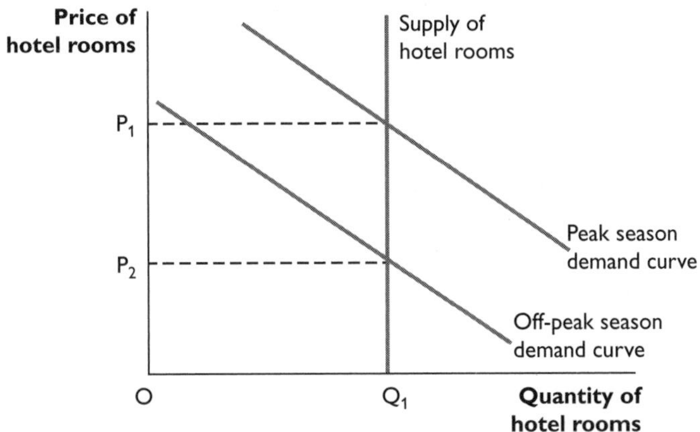

I am also assuming that hotels charge the equilibrium prices: P_1 in the peak season and P_2 in the off-peak. Higher prices are charged in the peak season because this is what the market will bear. The lower off-peak prices are also what the market bears, but there is another reason for low off-peak prices. The hotel rooms are there. Providing P_2 covers the extra cost of staffing, bed linen etc., letting the rooms at a low price can still be profitable. Letting the rooms at a low price is better (for the hotel) than having an empty room.

This is an excellent answer that scores full marks. The candidate has drawn a suitable diagram, labelling curves and axes accurately. His written answer complements the diagram very well. If there is a criticism, it is that his answer goes beyond the strict requirements of the question. **10/10 marks**

(e) Tourism can obviously help to raise the incomes of the inhabitants of poor countries such as Fiji. If tourism aids the processes of economic growth and development, it will have many advantages. However, economic growth and development are not the same thing. Growth can occur when, for example, foreign-based multinational leisure companies invest in beach resorts. But if the overseas-owned companies simply exploit the country in which they are operating, destroying the local culture and taking all the profits they make out of the country, growth takes place without proper economic development. Development is much more to do with improving, in a sustainable way, the conditions in which the population lives. Development involves improving the health and education of the indigenous population rather than just building a better road between hotels and airport to allow foreign tourists a quicker and more comfortable journey to and from their holiday destination. All too often rapid investment in tourist facilities has

destabilised local economies and cultures and has been against the long-term interest of native peoples. A few years ago when I went on holiday to Cyprus, I saw that people were refusing to work in vineyards picking grapes, preferring instead to work as waiters in the tourist hotels that were springing up. When I returned a year later, some of the vineyards had been abandoned whilst new and ugly hotels had been built on others. The local people working in the hotels were paid very low wages but the companies that own them were making millions of pounds by exploiting their workers.

Tourists themselves can also have an adverse effect. As a general rule, only rich or comparatively well-off people can afford to spend a holiday on an island like Fiji. Local people who see the wealth of their visitors become envious. Crime tends to grow in these circumstances. Some other tourist locations such as Ibiza attract young people from the UK who have a 'clubbing' culture. The visitors are not interested in the Spanish way of life in Ibiza, only in 'sun, sea, sex, drinking and drugs'. This has a bad effect on the island, and destroys Britain's reputation abroad.

e After a good start, this answer becomes too anecdotal and loses focus. The candidate seems to be arguing that the adverse effects of tourism exceed the benefits, except in the (comparatively rare) event of tourism promoting economic development as distinct from economic growth. The latter is a very good point to make. However, to earn a mark higher than Level 3 (7–9 marks), the candidate would have to set out possible benefits and adverse effects in a more structured way. The stimulus material in the question, especially in Extract C, provides quite a lot of prompts. The candidate has not made nearly as much use of this material as he might have. He should then *analyse* these effects, before *evaluating* or *assessing* their relative importance. As it is, he has not addressed sufficiently the key instruction in the question to explain why he agrees or disagrees with the assertion that the disadvantages of tourism exceed the advantages. With this type of question, he might argue that 'it all depends on circumstances'. Sometimes the disadvantages exceed the advantages, but not always. **7/15 marks**

Scored 28/40 70% = grade B

The music industry

Total for this question: 40 marks

Study **Extracts A**, **B** and **C**, and then answer **all** parts of the question which follows.

Extract A Music as a public good

The writing around the edge of a compact disc says *'All rights of the manufacturer and the owner of the recorded work reserved. Unauthorised copying, public performance and broadcasting of this record prohibited.'* This is an example of copyright, a part of intellectual property law that establishes the ownership and control of what is called non-tangible intellectual output. The two main examples are ideas (to which patents apply) and creativity (to which copyright applies). It is the latter that affects many sport and leisure industries such as the music and film industries.

Without such legal rights, which prevent performance and copying without permission, composers earn less than their music's market value — sometimes nothing at all. As a result, too few musical works are written or recorded.

Indeed, music is often a *public good* rather than a *private good*. Without copyright protection, pop songs and other musical compositions are available to anyone who cares to copy them free of charge. These people 'free-ride' on the effort of the original composer or pop group. Because of the 'free-rider' problem, market failure occurs.

In some circumstances, music is excludable, i.e. a performance can be given to a restricted, paying audience. Also, live performance of music may amount to rivalry: if I sit in front of you, you may get a worse view and/or a worse sound from the performance.

Extract B Selected statistics relating to the UK music industry, 1995

	£ million
Estimated value added by:	
Live performance	446.0
Other artists' earnings	525.0
Recording	415.4
Music publishing	85.5
Collection societies such as PRS	23.3
Retailing and distribution	334.1
Managers, agents and promoters	132.0
Other activities	539.9
Total	**2,501.2**
Total amount collected by collection societies such as the Performing Rights Society (PRS)	**346.1**

…oly and the music industry

… singers obviously want to prevent 'free-riding'. Because it is … an individual composer or pop singer to find out about every perform… his or her work and to arrange to collect the royalty, composers join the …erforming Rights Society (PRS), a membership organisation which monitors public performances, collects royalties and distributes them to its members. By protecting the composer via copyright law, the society confers a degree of monopoly power on composers. If they are successful enough, composers may use this monopoly power (or market power) to charge prices higher than the competitive level. This is a social cost of monopoly.

The PRS has a monopoly of administering performing rights: that is, the composer's or publisher's right to restrict and charge for public performance of their work. But following a complaint by the pop group U2 about alleged abuse of its monopoly power, in 1995 the PRS was investigated by the UK competition authorities. For the most part, the competition authorities found that the social benefits of the PRS's monopoly power exceed the social costs.

Source: all items adapted from an article by Ruth Towse in *The Economic Review*, November 1998.

(a) Distinguish between a 'public good' and a 'private good' (Extract A, line 11). (3 marks)

(b) Explain the statement 'because of the "free-rider" problem, market failure occurs' (Extract A, line 14). (4 marks)

(c) Explain ONE argument for and ONE argument against allowing people to record music free of charge without paying the composer or musician. (8 marks)

(d) With the help of a diagram, explain how monopoly may lead to higher prices than those charged in a competitive market (Extract C, lines 5–9). (10 marks)

(e) Making use of the data in Extract B and Extract C, assess the economic contribution of the Performing Rights Society to the music industry. (15 marks)

■ ■ ■

Candidate's answer

(a) (i) A private good such as a bar of chocolate is any good or service provided by a business in the private sector of the economy. By contrast, a public good such as state education is a good provided 'free' by the public sector and financed collectively by taxation.

e Unfortunately, this answer earns no marks. The candidate has made a very common error, confusing private goods with the private sector and public goods with the public sector. A public good, such as national defence or street lighting, is so called because if provided for one person, it is impossible to prevent other members of the general public from receiving its benefits. Because of this characteristic of *non-excludability*, markets generally fail to provide public goods; hence the case for alternative provision via public spending, financed collectively out of taxation. Public goods also have a second characteristic, *non-rivalry* or *non-diminishability*. By contrast, private goods (which markets can generally provide) have the opposite characteristics of *excludability* and *rivalry in consumption.* **0/3 marks**

(b) Market failure refers to any situation in which markets and the price mechanism function badly. There are various ways of classifying market failure. First, markets can function inequitably (unfairly) or inefficiently. In the latter case, allocative inefficiency occurs, i.e. a resource misallocation. Second, there can be complete market failure (leading to a 'missing market') or partial market failure. In the latter case, markets do provide a good, but they provide the 'wrong' or allocatively inefficient quantity: too much of a demerit good or too little of a merit good. A free-rider is someone who benefits without paying.

e The candidate scores a low mark because he misses the point of the question. In this case, the knowledge he displays is accurate but insufficiently addresses the set question. He writes a general account of market failure and accurately defines a 'free-rider'. To earn more than 1 mark, he must explain why 'free-riding' results in market failure. The explanation is linked to the next part of the question. When consumers can 'free-ride', they can consume a (public) good without paying. This causes the incentive function of prices to break down. The incentive for entrepreneurs to produce the public good for sale disappears, and markets fail to provide the public good. **1/4 marks**

(c) Until recently, most free recording involved analogue recording on audio cassette players. In recent years, however, many people have recorded music digitally on to their computers from the internet. The recorded music is of much higher quality and can be reproduced on 'pirate' CDs with no loss of quality, however many times it is reproduced. Internet businesses such as Napster came into existence to facilitate this type of recording. An argument in favour of allowing people to record music freely from the internet or from audio cassettes stems from the fact that, as Extract A indicates, music is often a public good. No extra costs are incurred by the composer, musician or recording company when music is copied in this way. If no costs are incurred, there is a case for as many people as possible to hear and enjoy the music. A second argument is that it is simply impractical to prevent people copying music for their own enjoyment. The main argument against, as the extracts also imply, is that every potential consumer has an incentive to 'free-ride', i.e. to benefit without paying. But if too many people decide to free-ride, there will be no incentive to record music in the first place, as composers, musicians and recording companies will no longer be able to make enough money from these activities.

e This answer earns full marks despite the fact that the candidate wastes time explaining some technical aspects of recording and copying music. Though interesting, this information is irrelevant and would be better left out. He also explains two arguments in favour of allowing people to record music without charge,

although the question only asks for one argument. No extra marks are awarded for going beyond the requirements of the question. More pleasingly, he resists the temptation to assess the relative merits of the arguments for and against. This part of the question asks for explanation, not evaluation. **8/8 marks**

(d) Compared to a competitive market, monopolies may exercise their market power to restrict output and raise the price charged to consumers. This power is greatest when demand is inelastic, as in my diagram below. In the diagram, the price charged by competitive firms is P_1. Q_1 is the output produced by all the firms. If competition is replaced by monopoly (i.e. one firm only in the market), the sole producer restricts output to Q_2 and hikes up the price to P_2. The monopoly may also restrict choice, and generally exploit consumers. Economists call this the exercise of 'producer sovereignty'. By contrast, in a competitive market the 'consumer is king'. This is 'consumer sovereignty'.

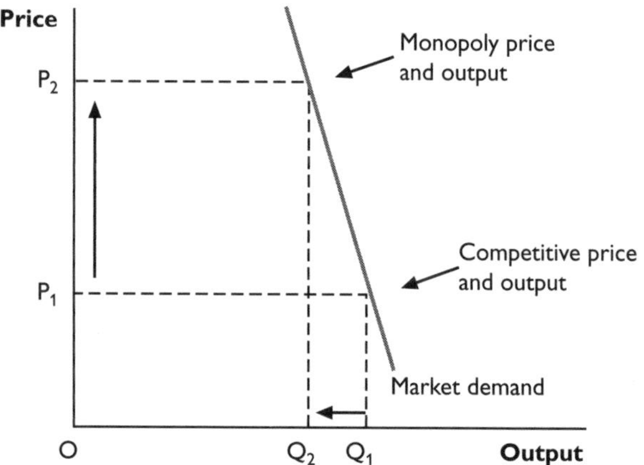

The candidate includes a certain amount of material not strictly relevant to the question (in this case, his explanation of producer sovereignty and consumer sovereignty). But he earns full marks because the rest of his answer addresses the set question and is completely accurate. His written answer complements his diagram very well indeed. **10/10 marks**

(e) Extract B shows that in 1995 the value added to the sales revenue generated by the UK music industry was £346.1 million, out of total sales revenue of £2,501.2 million. This is 13.8% of the total sales revenue earned by the music industry. This is a smaller figure than the amount earned by live performances (£446 million) and 'other earnings' (£525 million). This implies that composers, musicians and record companies could still earn a lot of money if the Performing Rights Society did not exist. However, they would not earn as much as they do, given the fact that the PRS collects royalties on their behalf. It is also possible that there would be much more 'free-riding' and music 'piracy' if the PRS did not exist.

A counter-argument is that the PRS only deals with activities such as radio stations and discos playing recorded music. It cannot prevent the mass pirating of recorded music over the internet that I described earlier. But perhaps the main argument against the PRS is that it is a monopoly, dictating the terms on which it distributes collected royalties to its members. Being a monopoly, it might be inefficient and charge too much for its services. But the PRS does save hugely on the transaction costs which individual musicians etc. would incur if each had to collect his or her own royalties.

Overall, I think that the advantages of the Performing Rights Society exceed any possible disadvantages. It has to have a huge network of inspectors to monitor use of live and broadcast music and a huge register of composers and their works for the distribution of royalties. There is a strong case for only one such organisation. Also, it permits the use of all its members' works for the price of one licence. This is fair because a local hairdresser pays much less for a PRS licence than a radio station. The monopoly power exercised by the PRS is generally beneficial. The organisation benefits from economies of scale and, by limiting to some extent the 'free-rider' problem, the PRS helps to keep the music industry commercially viable.

e This is an excellent answer, easily reaching Level 5 (13–15 marks) and in fact earning full marks. As instructed, the candidate makes good use of the data, and also brings in his own economic knowledge to address the issue posed by the question. The answer is particularly strong on evaluation. My only criticism is that the answer could have included more analysis and explanation of the points made. The candidate has finished the examination extremely strongly after a very weak start.

15/15 marks

Scored 34/40 85% = grade A